TEACHER'S PET PUBLICATIONS

PUZZLE PACK
for
The Giver

based on the book by
Lois Lowry

Written by
William T. Collins

© 2005 Teacher's Pet Publications
All Rights Reserved

The materials in this packet are copyrighted
by Teacher's Pet Publications, Inc.

These pages may be duplicated by the purchaser
for use in the purchaser's own classroom.

Copying any of these materials and distributing them
for any other purpose is a violation of the copyright laws.

© 2005 Teacher's Pet Publications, Inc.
www.tpet.com

INTRODUCTION
If you already own the LitPlan for this title, this Puzzle Pack will refresh your Unit Resource Materials and Vocabulary Resource Materials sections plus give you additional materials you can substitute into the tests. If you do not already have a complete LitPlan, these pages will give you some supplemental materials to use with your own plan. There are two main groups of materials: one set for unit words (such as characters' names, symbols, places, etc.) and one set for vocabulary words associated with the book.

WORD LIST
There is a word list for both the unit words and the vocabulary words. These lists show you which words are being used in the materials and the clues or definitions being used for those words. You may want to give students a word list with clues/definitions to help them, or you may want students to only have a word list (without clues/definitions) if you want them to work a little harder. Both are available for duplication. The word lists can also be your "calling key" for the bingo games.

FILL IN THE BLANK AND MATCHING
There are 4 each of the fill in the blank and matching worksheets for both the unit and vocabulary words. These pages can be used either as extra worksheets for students or as objective parts of a unit test. They can be done individually if students need extra help or as a whole class activity to review the material covered.

MAGIC SQUARES
The magic squares not only reinforce the material covered but also work on reasoning and math skills. Many teachers have told us that their students really enjoy doing these!

WORD SEARCH PUZZLES
The word search words go in all directions, as indicated on your answer keys. Two of the word search puzzles have the clues listed rather than the words. This makes the puzzle a little more difficult, but it reinforces the material better. Two word search puzzles have words only for students who find the clue puzzles too difficult.

CROSSWORD PUZZLES
Both unit and vocabulary word sections have 4 crossword puzzles.

BINGO CARDS
There are 32 individual bingo cards for the unit words and 32 individual bingo cards for the vocabulary words. You can use your word list as a "call list," calling the words at random and marking them off of your list as you go, or you could use the flash cards by cutting them apart and drawing the words at random from a hat (or box or whatever). To make a better review, you might ask for the definition and spelling of each word as you call it out—or you could call out the definitions and have students tell you the words they need to look for on the puzzle.

JUGGLE LETTERS
The vocabulary juggle letter game is intended to help students learn the spellings of the words. One sheet has the definitions listed on it as an extra help for students who need it or to reinforce the definitions if you choose to do so.

FLASH CARDS
We've included a set of vocabulary flash cards you can duplicate, cut, and fold for your students. Some teachers make a few sets for general use by the class; others make a set for each student. Some teachers duplicate them for each student and have the students cut & fold their own. You can cut out just the words and put them in a hat, have each student pick out one word and write the definition and a sentence for that word. Students then swap words and papers, with the next student adding a sentence of his own under the last one. You can have students swap as many times as you like. Each time the student will read the sentences written prior to his own and then add a sentence. You can cut out the words and definitions separately and play "I Have; Who Has?" Each student in the room draws a word and definition. The first student says, "I have (the name of the word). Who has the definition?" The student with the definition reads it then says, "I have (the name of the vocabulary word she has). Who has the definition?" The round continues until all words and definitions have been given.

The Giver Unit Word List

No.	Word	Clue/Definition
1.	AGE	Didn't matter after Ceremony of Twelve
2.	ANIMALS	None existed in Jonas's world
3.	APPLE	It changed before Jonas's eyes
4.	ASHER	Had trouble with language
5.	ASSIGNMENTS	The Elders chose these for the Twelves
6.	BACK	Jackets of Fours, Fives & Sixes buttoned down the ___
7.	BEYOND	Jonas was able to see ___
8.	BICYCLE	Moving out into the community
9.	BIRD	Gabe thought it was a plane
10.	BIRTHMOTHER	Not an honorable Assignment
11.	BOOKS	The Receiver had many in his dwelling
12.	CALCULATOR	Male Elevens' pants had a pocket for one
13.	CARETAKER	Fiona's assignment was ___ of the Old
14.	CHANGED	What happened to the apple
15.	CHIEF	Announced the assignments: ___ Elder
16.	COLORS	The people could not see them
17.	DECEMBER	Month of the Ceremony
18.	DISCIPLINE	This wand was a punishment tool for small children
19.	DISPOSITION	Father had a calmer one than Mother
20.	EIGHTS	Had jackets with small buttons and pockets
21.	ELEPHANT	Lily's comfort object
22.	ELSEWHERE	Outside the Community
23.	FEELINGS	Family shared them after dinner
24.	FEMALE	These Elevens new undergarments
25.	FIONA	Jonas dreamed about her
26.	GABRIEL	The newchild who stayed with Jonas
27.	GIVER	Transferred the memories to Jonas
28.	GRANDPARENTS	Jonas liked the memory of them
29.	HIPPO	Gabe's comfort object
30.	HONOR	The Receiver had this, but no power
31.	INDEPENDENCE	Jacket buttoned in front
32.	INTELLIGENCE	Mother's was higher than Father's
33.	JONAS	Became the new Receiver of Memory
34.	JUSTICE	Mother worked in this Department
35.	LANGUAGE	It was to be precise
36.	LARISSA	Described Roberto's ceremony
37.	LIE	Jonas, as Receiver, could do this
38.	LILY	Wanted to be a birthmother
39.	LOVE	Jonas asked his parents if they felt this for him
40.	MALE	These Elevens got longer pants with a pocket
41.	MATURITY	Short hair symbolized this
42.	MEMORIES	Jonas wanted to give them to people
43.	MOTHER	She was intelligent
44.	MUSIC	Jonas heard it coming from the bottom of the hill
45.	NAMING	Father broke a rule to look at this list
46.	NINES	They got their bicycles
47.	NINETEEN	Jonas's number
48.	NURTURER	Father's job
49.	OLD	Fiona worked in the House of the ___
50.	ONES	They got names and parents
51.	PAIN	The people had never known this
52.	PALE	Jonas's and Gabe's eyes looked this way
53.	PILL	Jonas stopped taking his

The Giver Unit Word List

No.	Word	Clue/Definition
54.	PLANES	Searched for Jonas and Gabe
55.	POWER	The Receiver did not have this
56.	RECEIVER	Jonas's Assignment was ___ of Memory
57.	RECREATION	Asher's Assignment was director of it
58.	RED	The color Jonas saw
59.	RELEASE	Jonas could not ask for this
60.	RIBBONS	Lily didn't like hair ___
61.	ROBERTO	Has a release ceremony in House of Old
62.	ROSEMARY	The Giver's daughter
63.	SAILING	This memory made Gabe go to sleep
64.	SAMENESS	People chose to go to it a long time ago
65.	SEVENS	Their jackets buttoned in front
66.	SLED	Jonas found one at the top of the hill
67.	SMACK	Asher confused it with snack
68.	STIRRINGS	Adults took daily pill for these
69.	TENS	They had their long hair cut off
70.	THREES	They learned language
71.	TWELVES	Got their adult Assignments
72.	TWINS	Father released the smaller of them
73.	WAR	Jonas recognized when the children played it

Copyrighted

The Giver Fill In The Blank 1

_____ 1. The color Jonas saw
_____ 2. They got names and parents
_____ 3. Father released the smaller of them
_____ 4. Gabe's comfort object
_____ 5. Searched for Jonas and Gabe
_____ 6. Transferred the memories to Jonas
_____ 7. Jonas heard it coming from the bottom of the hill
_____ 8. Family shared them after dinner
_____ 9. Mother's was higher than Father's
_____ 10. Short hair symbolized this
_____ 11. Father's job
_____ 12. Jonas stopped taking his
_____ 13. Lily didn't like hair ___
_____ 14. Moving out into the community
_____ 15. Gabe thought it was a plane
_____ 16. Jonas could not ask for this
_____ 17. They had their long hair cut off
_____ 18. Had jackets with small buttons and pockets
_____ 19. These Elevens got longer pants with a pocket
_____ 20. Jonas's Assignment was ___ of Memory

The Giver Fill In The Blank 1 Answer Key

RED	1. The color Jonas saw
ONES	2. They got names and parents
TWINS	3. Father released the smaller of them
HIPPO	4. Gabe's comfort object
PLANES	5. Searched for Jonas and Gabe
GIVER	6. Transferred the memories to Jonas
MUSIC	7. Jonas heard it coming from the bottom of the hill
FEELINGS	8. Family shared them after dinner
INTELLIGENCE	9. Mother's was higher than Father's
MATURITY	10. Short hair symbolized this
NURTURER	11. Father's job
PILL	12. Jonas stopped taking his
RIBBONS	13. Lily didn't like hair ___
BICYCLE	14. Moving out into the community
BIRD	15. Gabe thought it was a plane
RELEASE	16. Jonas could not ask for this
TENS	17. They had their long hair cut off
EIGHTS	18. Had jackets with small buttons and pockets
MALE	19. These Elevens got longer pants with a pocket
RECEIVER	20. Jonas's Assignment was ___ of Memory

Copyrighted

The Giver Fill In The Blank 2

_____ 1. The Receiver had this, but no power
_____ 2. Short hair symbolized this
_____ 3. The Elders chose these for the Twelves
_____ 4. The Receiver did not have this
_____ 5. Not an honorable Assignment
_____ 6. Jonas was able to see ___
_____ 7. Jonas dreamed about her
_____ 8. Gabe's comfort object
_____ 9. Described Roberto's ceremony
_____ 10. Male Elevens' pants had a pocket for one
_____ 11. They got their bicycles
_____ 12. This wand was a punishment tool for small children
_____ 13. Had trouble with language
_____ 14. Lily's comfort object
_____ 15. Father had a calmer one than Mother
_____ 16. Adults took daily pill for these
_____ 17. Jacket buttoned in front
_____ 18. It changed before Jonas's eyes
_____ 19. Month of the Ceremony
_____ 20. Lily didn't like hair ___

The Giver Fill In The Blank 2 Answer Key

HONOR	1. The Receiver had this, but no power
MATURITY	2. Short hair symbolized this
ASSIGNMENTS	3. The Elders chose these for the Twelves
POWER	4. The Receiver did not have this
BIRTHMOTHER	5. Not an honorable Assignment
BEYOND	6. Jonas was able to see ___
FIONA	7. Jonas dreamed about her
HIPPO	8. Gabe's comfort object
LARISSA	9. Described Roberto's ceremony
CALCULATOR	10. Male Elevens' pants had a pocket for one
NINES	11. They got their bicycles
DISCIPLINE	12. This wand was a punishment tool for small children
ASHER	13. Had trouble with language
ELEPHANT	14. Lily's comfort object
DISPOSITION	15. Father had a calmer one than Mother
STIRRINGS	16. Adults took daily pill for these
INDEPENDENCE	17. Jacket buttoned in front
APPLE	18. It changed before Jonas's eyes
DECEMBER	19. Month of the Ceremony
RIBBONS	20. Lily didn't like hair ___

The Giver Fill In The Blank 3

_____ 1. Jonas's number
_____ 2. Lily's comfort object
_____ 3. Searched for Jonas and Gabe
_____ 4. None existed in Jonas's world
_____ 5. She was intelligent
_____ 6. It was to be precise
_____ 7. They learned language
_____ 8. Got their adult Assignments
_____ 9. Mother worked in this Department
_____ 10. Father released the smaller of them
_____ 11. Father broke a rule to look at this list
_____ 12. Had jackets with small buttons and pockets
_____ 13. Jonas was able to see ___
_____ 14. People chose to go to it a long time ago
_____ 15. Asher confused it with snack
_____ 16. Jonas liked the memory of them
_____ 17. They got names and parents
_____ 18. Fiona's assignment was ___ of the Old
_____ 19. Jonas recognized when the children played it
_____ 20. Not an honorable Assignment

The Giver Fill In The Blank 3 Answer Key

NINETEEN	1. Jonas's number
ELEPHANT	2. Lily's comfort object
PLANES	3. Searched for Jonas and Gabe
ANIMALS	4. None existed in Jonas's world
MOTHER	5. She was intelligent
LANGUAGE	6. It was to be precise
THREES	7. They learned language
TWELVES	8. Got their adult Assignments
JUSTICE	9. Mother worked in this Department
TWINS	10. Father released the smaller of them
NAMING	11. Father broke a rule to look at this list
EIGHTS	12. Had jackets with small buttons and pockets
BEYOND	13. Jonas was able to see ___
SAMENESS	14. People chose to go to it a long time ago
SMACK	15. Asher confused it with snack
GRANDPARENTS	16. Jonas liked the memory of them
ONES	17. They got names and parents
CARETAKER	18. Fiona's assignment was ___ of the Old
WAR	19. Jonas recognized when the children played it
BIRTHMOTHER	20. Not an honorable Assignment

The Giver Fill In The Blank 4

1. The Receiver had many in his dwelling
2. The Elders chose these for the Twelves
3. Had trouble with language
4. Their jackets buttoned in front
5. They got their bicycles
6. Jonas recognized when the children played it
7. Jonas's and Gabe's eyes looked this way
8. What happened to the apple
9. The people had never known this
10. This memory made Gabe go to sleep
11. Asher's Assignment was director of it
12. Jacket buttoned in front
13. They learned language
14. Had jackets with small buttons and pockets
15. Didn't matter after Ceremony of Twelve
16. They had their long hair cut off
17. Wanted to be a birthmother
18. The Giver's daughter
19. Jonas wanted to give them to people
20. Got their adult Assignments

The Giver Fill In The Blank 4 Answer Key

BOOKS	1. The Receiver had many in his dwelling
ASSIGNMENTS	2. The Elders chose these for the Twelves
ASHER	3. Had trouble with language
SEVENS	4. Their jackets buttoned in front
NINES	5. They got their bicycles
WAR	6. Jonas recognized when the children played it
PALE	7. Jonas's and Gabe's eyes looked this way
CHANGED	8. What happened to the apple
PAIN	9. The people had never known this
SAILING	10. This memory made Gabe go to sleep
RECREATION	11. Asher's Assignment was director of it
INDEPENDENCE	12. Jacket buttoned in front
THREES	13. They learned language
EIGHTS	14. Had jackets with small buttons and pockets
AGE	15. Didn't matter after Ceremony of Twelve
TENS	16. They had their long hair cut off
LILY	17. Wanted to be a birthmother
ROSEMARY	18. The Giver's daughter
MEMORIES	19. Jonas wanted to give them to people
TWELVES	20. Got their adult Assignments

The Giver Matching 1

___ 1. CHANGED   A. The newchild who stayed with Jonas
___ 2. JUSTICE   B. None existed in Jonas's world
___ 3. HONOR   C. Gabe thought it was a plane
___ 4. ASSIGNMENTS   D. Month of the Ceremony
___ 5. NINES   E. Jonas could not ask for this
___ 6. ELSEWHERE   F. Lily's comfort object
___ 7. BICYCLE   G. The color Jonas saw
___ 8. BIRTHMOTHER   H. Jonas heard it coming from the bottom of the hill
___ 9. LANGUAGE   I. Jonas recognized when the children played it
___10. RED   J. Moving out into the community
___11. DECEMBER   K. The Receiver had many in his dwelling
___12. RELEASE   L. The Elders chose these for the Twelves
___13. BOOKS   M. Outside the Community
___14. BIRD   N. The Receiver had this, but no power
___15. ONES   O. It was to be precise
___16. ROBERTO   P. This wand was a punishment tool for small children
___17. PLANES   Q. Has a release ceremony in House of Old
___18. MUSIC   R. They got names and parents
___19. ELEPHANT   S. What happened to the apple
___20. WAR   T. Asher's Assignment was director of it
___21. STIRRINGS   U. Not an honorable Assignment
___22. ANIMALS   V. They got their bicycles
___23. DISCIPLINE   W. Adults took daily pill for these
___24. GABRIEL   X. Searched for Jonas and Gabe
___25. RECREATION   Y. Mother worked in this Department

The Giver Matching 1 Answer Key

S - 1. CHANGED	A.	The newchild who stayed with Jonas
Y - 2. JUSTICE	B.	None existed in Jonas's world
N - 3. HONOR	C.	Gabe thought it was a plane
L - 4. ASSIGNMENTS	D.	Month of the Ceremony
V - 5. NINES	E.	Jonas could not ask for this
M - 6. ELSEWHERE	F.	Lily's comfort object
J - 7. BICYCLE	G.	The color Jonas saw
U - 8. BIRTHMOTHER	H.	Jonas heard it coming from the bottom of the hill
O - 9. LANGUAGE	I.	Jonas recognized when the children played it
G -10. RED	J.	Moving out into the community
D -11. DECEMBER	K.	The Receiver had many in his dwelling
E -12. RELEASE	L.	The Elders chose these for the Twelves
K -13. BOOKS	M.	Outside the Community
C -14. BIRD	N.	The Receiver had this, but no power
R -15. ONES	O.	It was to be precise
Q -16. ROBERTO	P.	This wand was a punishment tool for small children
X -17. PLANES	Q.	Has a release ceremony in House of Old
H -18. MUSIC	R.	They got names and parents
F -19. ELEPHANT	S.	What happened to the apple
I -20. WAR	T.	Asher's Assignment was director of it
W -21. STIRRINGS	U.	Not an honorable Assignment
B -22. ANIMALS	V.	They got their bicycles
P -23. DISCIPLINE	W.	Adults took daily pill for these
A -24. GABRIEL	X.	Searched for Jonas and Gabe
T -25. RECREATION	Y.	Mother worked in this Department

The Giver Matching 2

___ 1. PALE   A. Mother worked in this Department
___ 2. SEVENS   B. Jonas dreamed about her
___ 3. INTELLIGENCE   C. It was to be precise
___ 4. RIBBONS   D. Moving out into the community
___ 5. LANGUAGE   E. Jonas was able to see ___
___ 6. LOVE   F. They learned language
___ 7. PILL   G. Jonas heard it coming from the bottom of the hill
___ 8. AGE   H. Jonas asked his parents if they felt this for him
___ 9. APPLE   I. Father's job
___10. CHANGED   J. Their jackets buttoned in front
___11. MUSIC   K. Male Elevens' pants had a pocket for one
___12. JUSTICE   L. This memory made Gabe go to sleep
___13. FIONA   M. Jonas stopped taking his
___14. THREES   N. What happened to the apple
___15. NAMING   O. Father broke a rule to look at this list
___16. LIE   P. Lily didn't like hair ___
___17. BEYOND   Q. Jonas, as Receiver, could do this
___18. BICYCLE   R. It changed before Jonas's eyes
___19. NINES   S. The newchild who stayed with Jonas
___20. COLORS   T. They got their bicycles
___21. MATURITY   U. Mother's was higher than Father's
___22. SAILING   V. Jonas's and Gabe's eyes looked this way
___23. NURTURER   W. Didn't matter after Ceremony of Twelve
___24. CALCULATOR   X. Short hair symbolized this
___25. GABRIEL   Y. The people could not see them

The Giver Matching 2 Answer Key

V - 1. PALE A. Mother worked in this Department
J - 2. SEVENS B. Jonas dreamed about her
U - 3. INTELLIGENCE C. It was to be precise
P - 4. RIBBONS D. Moving out into the community
C - 5. LANGUAGE E. Jonas was able to see ___
H - 6. LOVE F. They learned language
M - 7. PILL G. Jonas heard it coming from the bottom of the hill
W - 8. AGE H. Jonas asked his parents if they felt this for him
R - 9. APPLE I. Father's job
N -10. CHANGED J. Their jackets buttoned in front
G -11. MUSIC K. Male Elevens' pants had a pocket for one
A -12. JUSTICE L. This memory made Gabe go to sleep
B -13. FIONA M. Jonas stopped taking his
F -14. THREES N. What happened to the apple
O -15. NAMING O. Father broke a rule to look at this list
Q -16. LIE P. Lily didn't like hair ___
E -17. BEYOND Q. Jonas, as Receiver, could do this
D -18. BICYCLE R. It changed before Jonas's eyes
T -19. NINES S. The newchild who stayed with Jonas
Y -20. COLORS T. They got their bicycles
X -21. MATURITY U. Mother's was higher than Father's
L -22. SAILING V. Jonas's and Gabe's eyes looked this way
I -23. NURTURER W. Didn't matter after Ceremony of Twelve
K -24. CALCULATOR X. Short hair symbolized this
S -25. GABRIEL Y. The people could not see them

The Giver Matching 3

___ 1. SAILING   A. The Receiver had this, but no power
___ 2. RELEASE   B. Got their adult Assignments
___ 3. RIBBONS   C. Announced the assignments: ___ Elder
___ 4. DECEMBER   D. Lily's comfort object
___ 5. TENS   E. Short hair symbolized this
___ 6. ONES   F. Their jackets buttoned in front
___ 7. MEMORIES   G. Jonas recognized when the children played it
___ 8. CHIEF   H. The Elders chose these for the Twelves
___ 9. POWER   I. Lily didn't like hair ___
___10. HONOR   J. Father broke a rule to look at this list
___11. DISCIPLINE   K. Jonas's number
___12. DISPOSITION   L. Asher confused it with snack
___13. NAMING   M. This wand was a punishment tool for small children
___14. HIPPO   N. They got names and parents
___15. GABRIEL   O. Jonas could not ask for this
___16. ELEPHANT   P. Transferred the memories to Jonas
___17. TWELVES   Q. Father had a calmer one than Mother
___18. GIVER   R. Month of the Ceremony
___19. NINETEEN   S. Male Elevens' pants had a pocket for one
___20. CALCULATOR   T. The Receiver did not have this
___21. SEVENS   U. They had their long hair cut off
___22. SMACK   V. This memory made Gabe go to sleep
___23. WAR   W. The newchild who stayed with Jonas
___24. MATURITY   X. Gabe's comfort object
___25. ASSIGNMENTS   Y. Jonas wanted to give them to people

The Giver Matching 3 Answer Key

V - 1.	SAILING	A. The Receiver had this, but no power
O - 2.	RELEASE	B. Got their adult Assignments
I - 3.	RIBBONS	C. Announced the assignments: ___ Elder
R - 4.	DECEMBER	D. Lily's comfort object
U - 5.	TENS	E. Short hair symbolized this
N - 6.	ONES	F. Their jackets buttoned in front
Y - 7.	MEMORIES	G. Jonas recognized when the children played it
C - 8.	CHIEF	H. The Elders chose these for the Twelves
T - 9.	POWER	I. Lily didn't like hair ___
A - 10.	HONOR	J. Father broke a rule to look at this list
M - 11.	DISCIPLINE	K. Jonas's number
Q - 12.	DISPOSITION	L. Asher confused it with snack
J - 13.	NAMING	M. This wand was a punishment tool for small children
X - 14.	HIPPO	N. They got names and parents
W - 15.	GABRIEL	O. Jonas could not ask for this
D - 16.	ELEPHANT	P. Transferred the memories to Jonas
B - 17.	TWELVES	Q. Father had a calmer one than Mother
P - 18.	GIVER	R. Month of the Ceremony
K - 19.	NINETEEN	S. Male Elevens' pants had a pocket for one
S - 20.	CALCULATOR	T. The Receiver did not have this
F - 21.	SEVENS	U. They had their long hair cut off
L - 22.	SMACK	V. This memory made Gabe go to sleep
G - 23.	WAR	W. The newchild who stayed with Jonas
E - 24.	MATURITY	X. Gabe's comfort object
H - 25.	ASSIGNMENTS	Y. Jonas wanted to give them to people

The Giver Matching 4

___ 1. LILY   A. Jonas's and Gabe's eyes looked this way
___ 2. GABRIEL   B. Transferred the memories to Jonas
___ 3. NINES   C. They got their bicycles
___ 4. ONES   D. Jonas was able to see ___
___ 5. SAMENESS   E. They got names and parents
___ 6. LARISSA   F. Lily's comfort object
___ 7. SLED   G. The newchild who stayed with Jonas
___ 8. LOVE   H. Mother's was higher than Father's
___ 9. BICYCLE   I. Described Roberto's ceremony
___ 10. TWINS   J. Not an honorable Assignment
___ 11. RECEIVER   K. Father broke a rule to look at this list
___ 12. BEYOND   L. The Receiver had this, but no power
___ 13. NAMING   M. Jonas asked his parents if they felt this for him
___ 14. ROSEMARY   N. Father released the smaller of them
___ 15. PALE   O. Jonas stopped taking his
___ 16. INDEPENDENCE   P. Jonas's Assignment was ___ of Memory
___ 17. GIVER   Q. Moving out into the community
___ 18. ANIMALS   R. Jonas found one at the top of the hill
___ 19. PILL   S. Jonas, as Receiver, could do this
___ 20. ELEPHANT   T. The Giver's daughter
___ 21. INTELLIGENCE   U. Wanted to be a birthmother
___ 22. LIE   V. None existed in Jonas's world
___ 23. STIRRINGS   W. People chose to go to it a long time ago
___ 24. HONOR   X. Adults took daily pill for these
___ 25. BIRTHMOTHER   Y. Jacket buttoned in front

The Giver Matching 4 Answer Key

U -	1. LILY	A.	Jonas's and Gabe's eyes looked this way
G -	2. GABRIEL	B.	Transferred the memories to Jonas
C -	3. NINES	C.	They got their bicycles
E -	4. ONES	D.	Jonas was able to see ___
W -	5. SAMENESS	E.	They got names and parents
I -	6. LARISSA	F.	Lily's comfort object
R -	7. SLED	G.	The newchild who stayed with Jonas
M -	8. LOVE	H.	Mother's was higher than Father's
Q -	9. BICYCLE	I.	Described Roberto's ceremony
N -	10. TWINS	J.	Not an honorable Assignment
P -	11. RECEIVER	K.	Father broke a rule to look at this list
D -	12. BEYOND	L.	The Receiver had this, but no power
K -	13. NAMING	M.	Jonas asked his parents if they felt this for him
T -	14. ROSEMARY	N.	Father released the smaller of them
A -	15. PALE	O.	Jonas stopped taking his
Y -	16. INDEPENDENCE	P.	Jonas's Assignment was ___ of Memory
B -	17. GIVER	Q.	Moving out into the community
V -	18. ANIMALS	R.	Jonas found one at the top of the hill
O -	19. PILL	S.	Jonas, as Receiver, could do this
F -	20. ELEPHANT	T.	The Giver's daughter
H -	21. INTELLIGENCE	U.	Wanted to be a birthmother
S -	22. LIE	V.	None existed in Jonas's world
X -	23. STIRRINGS	W.	People chose to go to it a long time ago
L -	24. HONOR	X.	Adults took daily pill for these
J -	25. BIRTHMOTHER	Y.	Jacket buttoned in front

The Giver Magic Squares 1

Match the definition with the vocabulary word. Put your answers in the magic squares below. When your answers are correct, all columns and rows will add to the same number.

A. HONOR   E. EIGHTS   I. BICYCLE   M. BACK
B. CALCULATOR   F. ROSEMARY   J. SAILING   N. GIVER
C. LOVE   G. PALE   K. NAMING   O. BIRD
D. FIONA   H. LIE   L. CARETAKER   P. OLD

1. Gabe thought it was a plane
2. Jonas dreamed about her
3. This memory made Gabe go to sleep
4. Had jackets with small buttons and pockets
5. Moving out into the community
6. The Giver's daughter
7. Fiona worked in the House of the ___
8. Jonas asked his parents if they felt this for him
9. Jonas, as Receiver, could do this
10. Father broke a rule to look at this list
11. The Receiver had this, but no power
12. Transferred the memories to Jonas
13. Male Elevens' pants had a pocket for one
14. Jackets of Fours, Fives & Sixes buttoned down the ___
15. Jonas's and Gabe's eyes looked this way
16. Fiona's assignment was ___ of the Old

A=	B=	C=	D=
E=	F=	G=	H=
I=	J=	K=	L=
M=	N=	O=	P=

The Giver Magic Squares 1 Answer Key

Match the definition with the vocabulary word. Put your answers in the magic squares below. When your answers are correct, all columns and rows will add to the same number.

A. HONOR
B. CALCULATOR
C. LOVE
D. FIONA
E. EIGHTS
F. ROSEMARY
G. PALE
H. LIE
I. BICYCLE
J. SAILING
K. NAMING
L. CARETAKER
M. BACK
N. GIVER
O. BIRD
P. OLD

1. Gabe thought it was a plane
2. Jonas dreamed about her
3. This memory made Gabe go to sleep
4. Had jackets with small buttons and pockets
5. Moving out into the community
6. The Giver's daughter
7. Fiona worked in the House of the ___
8. Jonas asked his parents if they felt this for him
9. Jonas, as Receiver, could do this
10. Father broke a rule to look at this list
11. The Receiver had this, but no power
12. Transferred the memories to Jonas
13. Male Elevens' pants had a pocket for one
14. Jackets of Fours, Fives & Sixes buttoned down the ___
15. Jonas's and Gabe's eyes looked this way
16. Fiona's assignment was ___ of the Old

A=11	B=13	C=8	D=2
E=4	F=6	G=15	H=9
I=5	J=3	K=10	L=16
M=14	N=12	O=1	P=7

The Giver Magic Squares 2

Match the definition with the vocabulary word. Put your answers in the magic squares below. When your answers are correct, all columns and rows will add to the same number.

A. AGE
B. BEYOND
C. TENS
D. CHIEF
E. ELEPHANT
F. CARETAKER
G. OLD
H. RELEASE
I. PILL
J. WAR
K. BACK
L. NINETEEN
M. SEVENS
N. ASHER
O. STIRRINGS
P. GIVER

1. Jonas could not ask for this
2. Their jackets buttoned in front
3. Jonas was able to see ___
4. Jackets of Fours, Fives & Sixes buttoned down the ___
5. Jonas recognized when the children played it
6. They had their long hair cut off
7. Transferred the memories to Jonas
8. Lily's comfort object
9. Adults took daily pill for these
10. Fiona's assignment was ___ of the Old
11. Jonas stopped taking his
12. Announced the assignments: ___ Elder
13. Didn't matter after Ceremony of Twelve
14. Jonas's number
15. Fiona worked in the House of the ___
16. Had trouble with language

A=	B=	C=	D=
E=	F=	G=	H=
I=	J=	K=	L=
M=	N=	O=	P=

The Giver Magic Squares 2 Answer Key

Match the definition with the vocabulary word. Put your answers in the magic squares below. When your answers are correct, all columns and rows will add to the same number.

A. AGE
B. BEYOND
C. TENS
D. CHIEF
E. ELEPHANT
F. CARETAKER
G. OLD
H. RELEASE
I. PILL
J. WAR
K. BACK
L. NINETEEN
M. SEVENS
N. ASHER
O. STIRRINGS
P. GIVER

1. Jonas could not ask for this
2. Their jackets buttoned in front
3. Jonas was able to see ___
4. Jackets of Fours, Fives & Sixes buttoned down the ___
5. Jonas recognized when the children played it
6. They had their long hair cut off
7. Transferred the memories to Jonas
8. Lily's comfort object
9. Adults took daily pill for these
10. Fiona's assignment was ___ of the Old
11. Jonas stopped taking his
12. Announced the assignments: ___ Elder
13. Didn't matter after Ceremony of Twelve
14. Jonas's number
15. Fiona worked in the House of the ___
16. Had trouble with language

A=13	B=3	C=6	D=12
E=8	F=10	G=15	H=1
I=11	J=5	K=4	L=14
M=2	N=16	O=9	P=7

The Giver Magic Squares 3

Match the definition with the vocabulary word. Put your answers in the magic squares below. When your answers are correct, all columns and rows will add to the same number.

A. MATURITY   E. NINETEEN   I. ROSEMARY   M. ROBERTO
B. ASSIGNMENTS   F. TWELVES   J. BEYOND   N. RELEASE
C. CALCULATOR   G. DECEMBER   K. PLANES   O. MALE
D. BOOKS   H. INDEPENDENCE   L. GIVER   P. PALE

1. Jacket buttoned in front
2. Short hair symbolized this
3. The Elders chose these for the Twelves
4. Month of the Ceremony
5. Jonas was able to see ___
6. These Elevens got longer pants with a pocket
7. Jonas's and Gabe's eyes looked this way
8. The Giver's daughter
9. Searched for Jonas and Gabe
10. Jonas could not ask for this
11. Has a release ceremony in House of Old
12. Transferred the memories to Jonas
13. Jonas's number
14. The Receiver had many in his dwelling
15. Male Elevens' pants had a pocket for one
16. Got their adult Assignments

A=	B=	C=	D=
E=	F=	G=	H=
I=	J=	K=	L=
M=	N=	O=	P=

The Giver Magic Squares 3 Answer Key

Match the definition with the vocabulary word. Put your answers in the magic squares below. When your answers are correct, all columns and rows will add to the same number.

A. MATURITY   E. NINETEEN   I. ROSEMARY   M. ROBERTO
B. ASSIGNMENTS F. TWELVES   J. BEYOND   N. RELEASE
C. CALCULATOR G. DECEMBER   K. PLANES   O. MALE
D. BOOKS   H. INDEPENDENCE   L. GIVER   P. PALE

1. Jacket buttoned in front
2. Short hair symbolized this
3. The Elders chose these for the Twelves
4. Month of the Ceremony
5. Jonas was able to see ___
6. These Elevens got longer pants with a pocket
7. Jonas's and Gabe's eyes looked this way
8. The Giver's daughter
9. Searched for Jonas and Gabe
10. Jonas could not ask for this
11. Has a release ceremony in House of Old
12. Transferred the memories to Jonas
13. Jonas's number
14. The Receiver had many in his dwelling
15. Male Elevens' pants had a pocket for one
16. Got their adult Assignments

A=2	B=3	C=15	D=14
E=13	F=16	G=4	H=1
I=8	J=5	K=9	L=12
M=11	N=10	O=6	P=7

The Giver Magic Squares 4

Match the definition with the vocabulary word. Put your answers in the magic squares below. When your answers are correct, all columns and rows will add to the same number.

A. RECEIVER
B. NAMING
C. APPLE
D. BIRTHMOTHER
E. STIRRINGS
F. JONAS
G. SAMENESS
H. ELSEWHERE
I. CARETAKER
J. GABRIEL
K. CHIEF
L. PAIN
M. ASSIGNMENTS
N. INTELLIGENCE
O. CALCULATOR
P. HIPPO

1. The Elders chose these for the Twelves
2. Became the new Receiver of Memory
3. Outside the Community
4. Male Elevens' pants had a pocket for one
5. The people had never known this
6. It changed before Jonas's eyes
7. Jonas's Assignment was ___ of Memory
8. The newchild who stayed with Jonas
9. Announced the assignments: ___ Elder
10. Not an honorable Assignment
11. Father broke a rule to look at this list
12. Fiona's assignment was ___ of the Old
13. Mother's was higher than Father's
14. Adults took daily pill for these
15. People chose to go to it a long time ago
16. Gabe's comfort object

A=	B=	C=	D=
E=	F=	G=	H=
I=	J=	K=	L=
M=	N=	O=	P=

The Giver Magic Squres 4 Answer Key

Match the definition with the vocabulary word. Put your answers in the magic squares below. When your answers are correct, all columns and rows will add to the same number.

A. RECEIVER   E. STIRRINGS   I. CARETAKER   M. ASSIGNMENTS
B. NAMING   F. JONAS   J. GABRIEL   N. INTELLIGENCE
C. APPLE   G. SAMENESS   K. CHIEF   O. CALCULATOR
D. BIRTHMOTHER   H. ELSEWHERE   L. PAIN   P. HIPPO

1. The Elders chose these for the Twelves
2. Became the new Receiver of Memory
3. Outside the Community
4. Male Elevens' pants had a pocket for one
5. The people had never known this
6. It changed before Jonas's eyes
7. Jonas's Assignment was ___ of Memory
8. The newchild who stayed with Jonas
9. Announced the assignments: ___ Elder
10. Not an honorable Assignment
11. Father broke a rule to look at this list
12. Fiona's assignment was ___ of the Old
13. Mother's was higher than Father's
14. Adults took daily pill for these
15. People chose to go to it a long time ago
16. Gabe's comfort object

A=7	B=11	C=6	D=10
E=14	F=2	G=15	H=3
I=12	J=8	K=9	L=5
M=1	N=13	O=4	P=16

The Giver Word Search 1

```
H I P P O I R E V I G P S S M A C K
C R C F I E N O I A F A L L Z P T Q
M O Q V W L F T B G M L Y A W P E Z
V T L O G Y L R E E H E F M N L N Y
W A P O Y L I F N L R T V I C E N S L
I L H H R E R E D E L T S N O N S F
N U B T L S S I S P B I O A O N E D
D C M A W S L H T H M G B B B E A B
E L C Y C I B C N A C A B E L H S B
P A I L L K N L E N S I L I N K H T
E C S Y Q J A S R T R H N E O C L B
N X U T R N S A A K V G E O G V E V
D L M M G E S Z P T S K B R N C F N
E P O U F S L R D E N Y D W I E J T
N R A V I N N E N M B E E T M P O K
C G E R E Q H I A I L O I A A D N R
E G A D H O N O R S A I L I N G A W
T L O N E S S D G P E E N D C W S N
```

- Announced the assignments: ___ Elder (5)
- Asher confused it with snack (5)
- Became the new Receiver of Memory (5)
- Described Roberto's ceremony (7)
- Didn't matter after Ceremony of Twelve (3)
- Family shared them after dinner (8)
- Father broke a rule to look at this list (6)
- Father released the smaller of them (5)
- Fiona worked in the House of the ___ (3)
- Gabe thought it was a plane (4)
- Gabe's comfort object (5)
- Had jackets with small buttons and pockets (6)
- Had trouble with language (5)
- Has a release ceremony in House of Old (7)
- It changed before Jonas's eyes (5)
- It was to be precise (8)
- Jacket buttoned in front (12)
- Jackets of Fours, Fives & Sixes buttoned down the ___ (4)
- Jonas asked his parents if they felt this for him (4)
- Jonas could not ask for this (7)
- Jonas dreamed about her (5)
- Jonas found one at the top of the hill (4)
- Jonas heard it coming from the bottom of the hill (5)
- Jonas liked the memory of them (12)
- Jonas recognized when the children played it (3)
- Jonas stopped taking his (4)
- Jonas's and Gabe's eyes looked this way (4)
- Jonas, as Receiver, could do this (3)
- Lily didn't like hair ___ (7)
- Lily's comfort object (8)
- Male Elevens' pants had a pocket for one (10)
- Mother's was higher than Father's (12)
- Moving out into the community (7)
- None existed in Jonas's world (7)
- People chose to go to it a long time ago (8)
- Searched for Jonas and Gabe (6)
- The Receiver did not have this (5)
- The Receiver had many in his dwelling (5)
- The Receiver had this, but no power (5)
- The color Jonas saw (3)
- The newchild who stayed with Jonas (7)
- The people could not see them (6)
- The people had never known this (4)
- These Elevens got longer pants with a pocket (4)
- These Elevens new undergarments (6)
- They got names and parents (4)
- They got their bicycles (5)
- They had their long hair cut off (4)
- This memory made Gabe go to sleep (7)
- Transferred the memories to Jonas (5)
- Wanted to be a birthmother (4)

The Giver Word Search 1 Answer Key

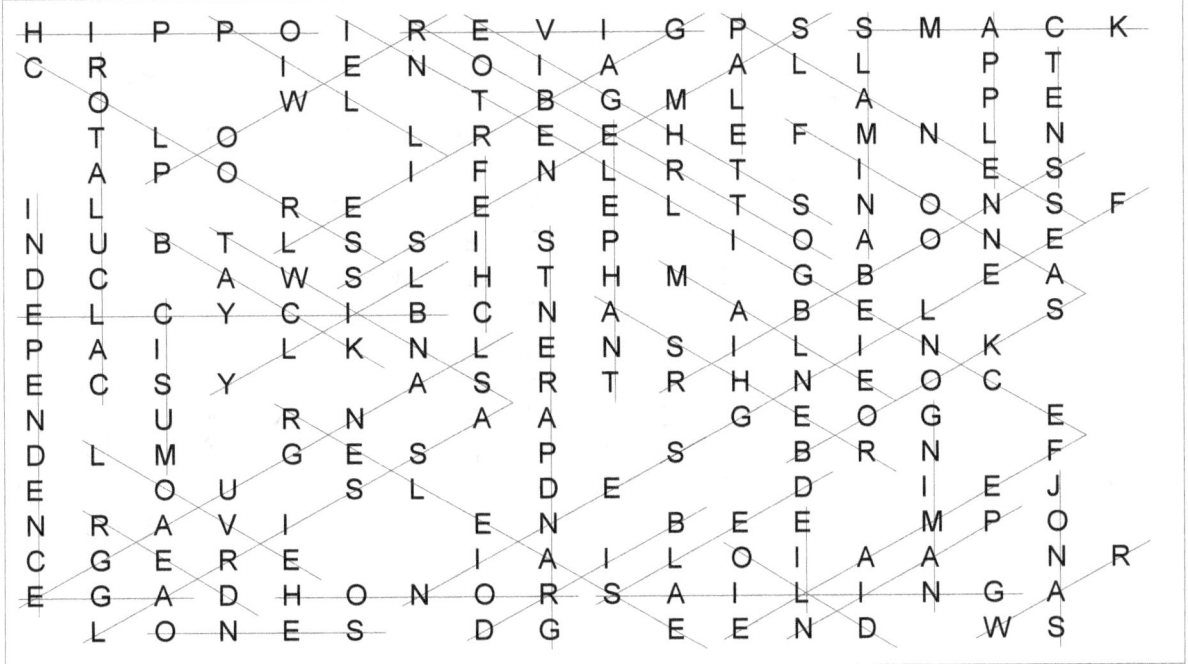

- Announced the assignments: ___ Elder (5)
- Asher confused it with snack (5)
- Became the new Receiver of Memory (5)
- Described Roberto's ceremony (7)
- Didn't matter after Ceremony of Twelve (3)
- Family shared them after dinner (8)
- Father broke a rule to look at this list (6)
- Father released the smaller of them (5)
- Fiona worked in the House of the ___ (3)
- Gabe thought it was a plane (4)
- Gabe's comfort object (5)
- Had jackets with small buttons and pockets (6)
- Had trouble with language (5)
- Has a release ceremony in House of Old (7)
- It changed before Jonas's eyes (5)
- It was to be precise (8)
- Jacket buttoned in front (12)
- Jackets of Fours, Fives & Sixes buttoned down the ___ (4)
- Jonas asked his parents if they felt this for him (4)
- Jonas could not ask for this (7)
- Jonas dreamed about her (5)
- Jonas found one at the top of the hill (4)
- Jonas heard it coming from the bottom of the hill (5)
- Jonas liked the memory of them (12)
- Jonas recognized when the children played it (3)
- Jonas stopped taking his (4)
- Jonas's and Gabe's eyes looked this way (4)
- Jonas, as Receiver, could do this (3)
- Lily didn't like hair ___ (7)
- Lily's comfort object (8)
- Male Elevens' pants had a pocket for one (10)
- Mother's was higher than Father's (12)
- Moving out into the community (7)
- None existed in Jonas's world (7)
- People chose to go to it a long time ago (8)
- Searched for Jonas and Gabe (6)
- The Receiver did not have this (5)
- The Receiver had many in his dwelling (5)
- The Receiver had this, but no power (5)
- The color Jonas saw (3)
- The newchild who stayed with Jonas (7)
- The people could not see them (6)
- The people had never known this (4)
- These Elevens got longer pants with a pocket (4)
- These Elevens new undergarments (6)
- They got names and parents (4)
- They got their bicycles (5)
- They had their long hair cut off (4)
- This memory made Gabe go to sleep (7)
- Transferred the memories to Jonas (5)
- Wanted to be a birthmother (4)

The Giver Word Search 2

```
R I B B O N S D S A M E N E S S W T
O T W E L V E S H L G L H S M A C K
S Q L Z G L D C A A N A O B C N F L
E A H Y S E S N U R I M N I B O E W
M P J C G A O G F I N E O R K J E H
A S N N I I N C G S E F R D F H L W
R V A L F A O A F S T E P O B L I K
Y H I D L L L S Z A E L W O N H N G
C N S E O R B H G T E P Z N W E G F
G A B R I E L E N L N P L A N E S C
M I S S K S V R Y A X A A G I E R B
U J V B N O T E Z O M R Y L N W V X
S R Q E L H L H D P N I O I E D Q F
I T V D R O C W F N T D N B O O K S
C E P E P H Z E L V W T I G E C P C
S Z E P M D I S L L I E A X A R R M
L S I N L H Y L I L N N P B Y A T Y
L H P O C T K E P M S S D Y W D S O
```

Announced the assignments: ___ Elder (5)
Asher confused it with snack (5)
Became the new Receiver of Memory (5)
Described Roberto's ceremony (7)
Didn't matter after Ceremony of Twelve (3)
Family shared them after dinner (8)
Father broke a rule to look at this list (6)
Father released the smaller of them (5)
Fiona worked in the House of the ___ (3)
Gabe thought it was a plane (4)
Gabe's comfort object (5)
Got their adult Assignments (7)
Had trouble with language (5)
Has a release ceremony in House of Old (7)
It changed before Jonas's eyes (5)
It was to be precise (8)
Jackets of Fours, Fives & Sixes buttoned down the ___ (4)
Jonas asked his parents if they felt this for him (4)
Jonas dreamed about her (5)
Jonas found one at the top of the hill (4)
Jonas heard it coming from the bottom of the hill (5)
Jonas recognized when the children played it (3)
Jonas stopped taking his (4)
Jonas was able to see ___ (6)

Jonas's and Gabe's eyes looked this way (4)
Jonas's number (8)
Jonas, as Receiver, could do this (3)
Lily didn't like hair ___ (7)
Outside the Community (9)
People chose to go to it a long time ago (8)
Searched for Jonas and Gabe (6)
The Giver's daughter (8)
The Receiver did not have this (5)
The Receiver had many in his dwelling (5)
The Receiver had this, but no power (5)
The color Jonas saw (3)
The newchild who stayed with Jonas (7)
The people could not see them (6)
The people had never known this (4)
Their jackets buttoned in front (6)
These Elevens got longer pants with a pocket (4)
These Elevens new undergarments (6)
They got names and parents (4)
They got their bicycles (5)
They had their long hair cut off (4)
They learned language (6)
This memory made Gabe go to sleep (7)
Transferred the memories to Jonas (5)
Wanted to be a birthmother (4)
What happened to the apple (7)

The Giver Word Search 2 Answer Key

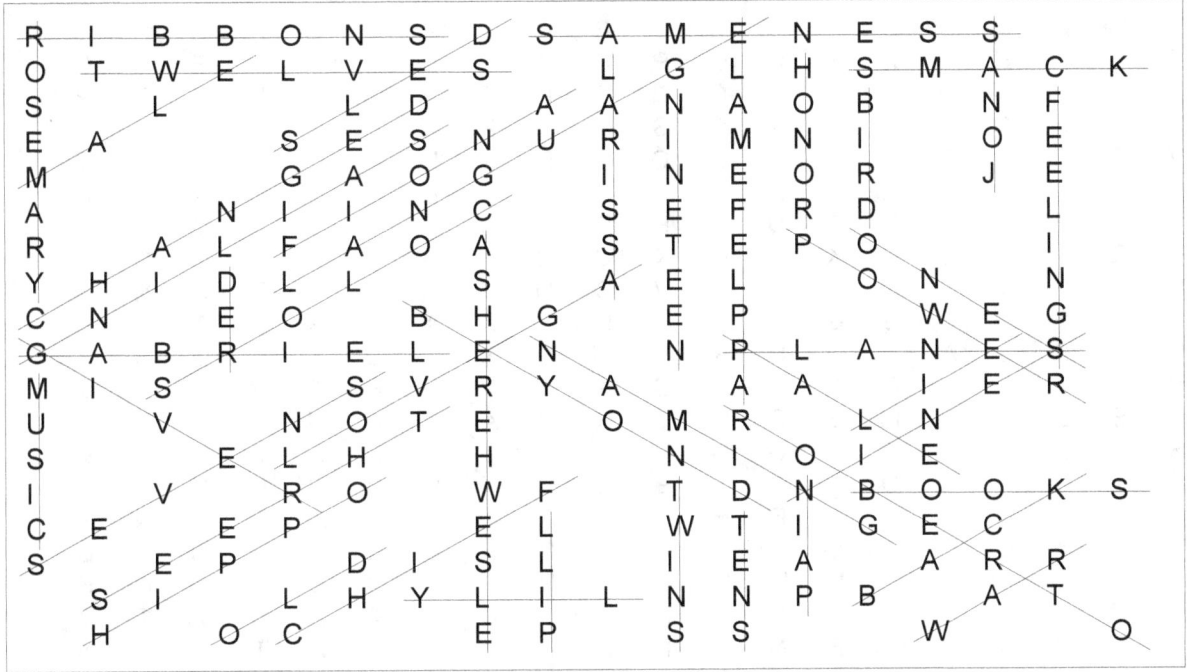

Announced the assignments: ___ Elder (5)
Asher confused it with snack (5)
Became the new Receiver of Memory (5)
Described Roberto's ceremony (7)
Didn't matter after Ceremony of Twelve (3)
Family shared them after dinner (8)
Father broke a rule to look at this list (6)
Father released the smaller of them (5)
Fiona worked in the House of the ___ (3)
Gabe thought it was a plane (4)
Gabe's comfort object (5)
Got their adult Assignments (7)
Had trouble with language (5)
Has a release ceremony in House of Old (7)
It changed before Jonas's eyes (5)
It was to be precise (8)
Jackets of Fours, Fives & Sixes buttoned down the ___ (4)
Jonas asked his parents if they felt this for him (4)
Jonas dreamed about her (5)
Jonas found one at the top of the hill (4)
Jonas heard it coming from the bottom of the hill (5)
Jonas recognized when the children played it (3)
Jonas stopped taking his (4)
Jonas was able to see ___ (6)

Jonas's and Gabe's eyes looked this way (4)
Jonas's number (8)
Jonas, as Receiver, could do this (3)
Lily didn't like hair ___ (7)
Outside the Community (9)
People chose to go to it a long time ago (8)
Searched for Jonas and Gabe (6)
The Giver's daughter (8)
The Receiver did not have this (5)
The Receiver had many in his dwelling (5)
The Receiver had this, but no power (5)
The color Jonas saw (3)
The newchild who stayed with Jonas (7)
The people could not see them (6)
The people had never known this (4)
Their jackets buttoned in front (6)
These Elevens got longer pants with a pocket (4)
These Elevens new undergarments (6)
They got names and parents (4)
They got their bicycles (5)
They had their long hair cut off (4)
They learned language (6)
This memory made Gabe go to sleep (7)
Transferred the memories to Jonas (5)
Wanted to be a birthmother (4)
What happened to the apple (7)

The Giver Word Search 3

```
T W X M U S I C A L C U L A T O R O R S
W B F E W F S H A G R P W B E V P E B C
E V R M D F S A O Q C E T E C P R C D R
L J R O P L A N E S Y X K K I U P I L L
V F E R C X O G S O Q E X H T G F Y G V
E G C I H H Y E N F L I Y R S L H N N P
S B E E I F G D G B R L U T U I I T Y S
E B I S E N K T I X O N A B J L B T S G
V A V J F G E S V V S O V R I Y I R N T
E C E D O S G L E D E T K A I R E Z I G
N K R L A N G L R E M D S S U S L Z N G
S I T E I Z A G Y C A Y M T R T S N E Y
B S L L Q M B S G E R B A P I N E A T V
S E E W E F R G H M Y M C C B E W M E G
R E L F T Q I G T B C C K W B R H I E W
F L C E N Z E F H E V A J P O A E N N R
W A Y C P I L R R R C P R L N P R G I F
M N C P V H N W E O F P J E S D E O L D
P G I Q B D A E E J B L D V T N N W Z F
R U B M P T E N S P R E C R E A T I O Y
B A H O Y L M R T P G M R P F R K D T N
Z G W T S R O Z W A X A D T A G N E S S
R E H S A L A N I M A L S C O I D E R S
R N L W O F E N N X O E S A M E N E S C
F G K C R E D D S M O T H E R O P A L E
```

AGE	ELSEWHERE	MATURITY	RED
ANIMALS	FEELINGS	MEMORIES	RELEASE
APPLE	FEMALE	MOTHER	RIBBONS
ASHER	FIONA	MUSIC	ROBERTO
BACK	GABRIEL	NAMING	ROSEMARY
BEYOND	GIVER	NINES	SAILING
BICYCLE	GRANDPARENTS	NINETEEN	SAMENESS
BIRD	HIPPO	NURTURER	SEVENS
BOOKS	HONOR	OLD	SLED
CALCULATOR	JONAS	ONES	SMACK
CARETAKER	JUSTICE	PAIN	TENS
CHANGED	LANGUAGE	PALE	THREES
CHIEF	LARISSA	PILL	TWELVES
COLORS	LIE	PLANES	TWINS
DECEMBER	LILY	POWER	WAR
EIGHTS	LOVE	RECEIVER	
ELEPHANT	MALE	RECREATION	

Copyrighted

The Giver Word Search 3 Answer Key

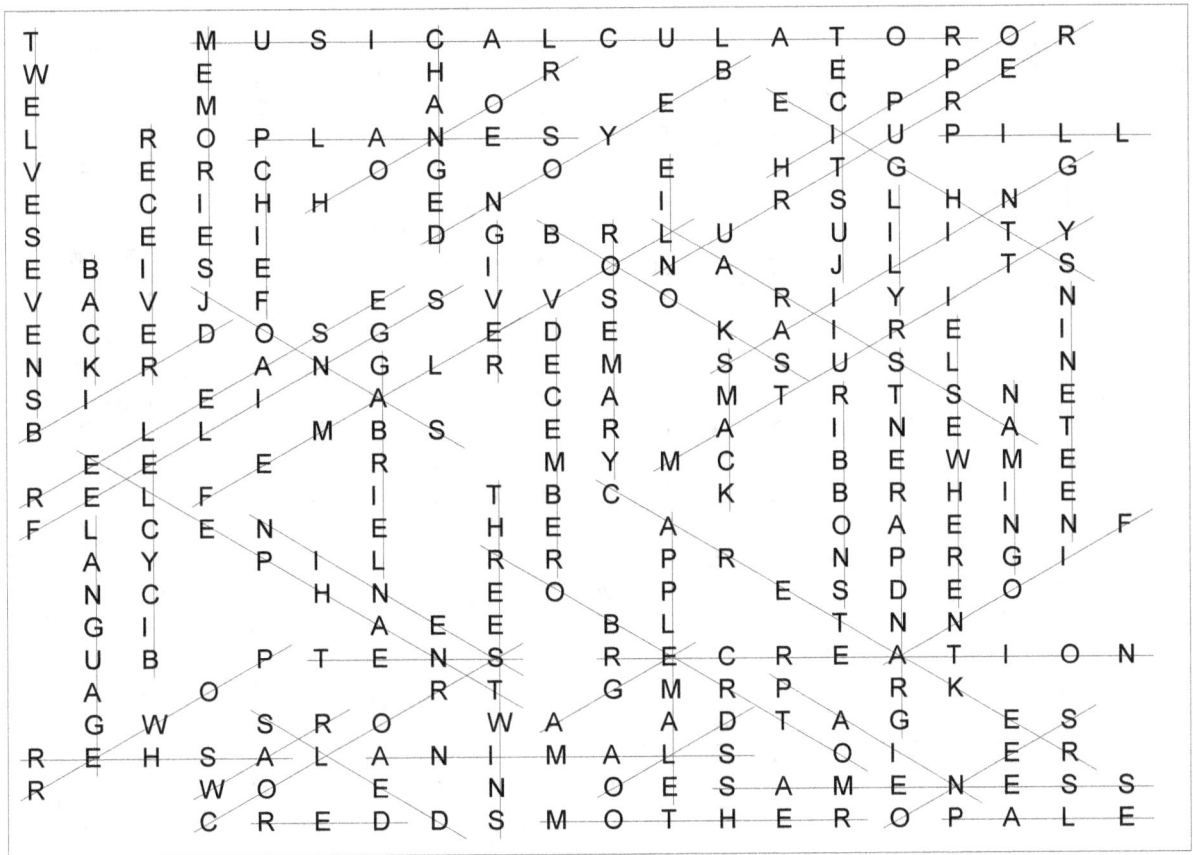

AGE	ELSEWHERE	MATURITY	RED
ANIMALS	FEELINGS	MEMORIES	RELEASE
APPLE	FEMALE	MOTHER	RIBBONS
ASHER	FIONA	MUSIC	ROBERTO
BACK	GABRIEL	NAMING	ROSEMARY
BEYOND	GIVER	NINES	SAILING
BICYCLE	GRANDPARENTS	NINETEEN	SAMENESS
BIRD	HIPPO	NURTURER	SEVENS
BOOKS	HONOR	OLD	SLED
CALCULATOR	JONAS	ONES	SMACK
CARETAKER	JUSTICE	PAIN	TENS
CHANGED	LANGUAGE	PALE	THREES
CHIEF	LARISSA	PILL	TWELVES
COLORS	LIE	PLANES	TWINS
DECEMBER	LILY	POWER	WAR
EIGHTS	LOVE	RECEIVER	
ELEPHANT	MALE	RECREATION	

The Giver Word Search 4

```
S A I L I N G R I B O N S L L T S B P
C S M L A N G U A G E X F I O A E M O F
T A A E S E W H E R E L C V R N A O M
W M T G S A P G E R Y B L E I S C K Z
E E U J X R C P G W M W S P V S V K S F
L N R M V O S G N I L E E F S S C T L T
V E I D F L C A I K T H N Q S A H E H Y
E S T H E O E G M N F O I T Q G I R W H
S S Y R E C R E A T I O N R I R E D R J
P T A W I R E H N B K E K E B E F O E P
N W V T B G P M N Z M T F A S K T B C M
M N S D S E R P B N Y M G C K A F I E B
B U P I L L J A G E O L D C L T E R I C
J R S E S R P I N T R L A U M E M D V G
R T A I K T S N H D Z B C C V R A H E V
F U N P C S I E P M P L C Y D A L I R V
G R O A A B R R P O A A N H S C E P R D
B E J L S S O E R C W L R L A J I P G M
M R R E N B N V P I M E E N N L O T F
V V F E E Y O I L B N D R L N G K R G
N Q V R E X H G A E Q G T C G T Y E R X
S E T L M C K N N Y H W S Y W C S E D P
S O P M D M O Q E O I C B C G T H R S Z
C P F K N I F W S N R N J I F S D Y B N
A W V T F G K T S D K F L B A J V W J N
```

AGE	ELEPHANT	LOVE	RECREATION
APPLE	ELSEWHERE	MALE	RED
ASHER	FEELINGS	MATURITY	RELEASE
ASSIGNMENTS	FEMALE	MOTHER	RIBBONS
BACK	FIONA	MUSIC	ROBERTO
BEYOND	GABRIEL	NAMING	SAILING
BICYCLE	GIVER	NINES	SAMENESS
BIRD	GRANDPARENTS	NURTURER	SEVENS
BOOKS	HIPPO	OLD	SLED
CALCULATOR	HONOR	ONES	SMACK
CARETAKER	JONAS	PAIN	STIRRINGS
CHANGED	JUSTICE	PALE	TENS
CHIEF	LANGUAGE	PILL	THREES
COLORS	LARISSA	PLANES	TWELVES
DECEMBER	LIE	POWER	TWINS
EIGHTS	LILY	RECEIVER	WAR

The Giver Word Search 4 Answer Key

AGE	ELEPHANT	LOVE	RECREATION
APPLE	ELSEWHERE	MALE	RED
ASHER	FEELINGS	MATURITY	RELEASE
ASSIGNMENTS	FEMALE	MOTHER	RIBBONS
BACK	FIONA	MUSIC	ROBERTO
BEYOND	GABRIEL	NAMING	SAILING
BICYCLE	GIVER	NINES	SAMENESS
BIRD	GRANDPARENTS	NURTURER	SEVENS
BOOKS	HIPPO	OLD	SLED
CALCULATOR	HONOR	ONES	SMACK
CARETAKER	JONAS	PAIN	STIRRINGS
CHANGED	JUSTICE	PALE	TENS
CHIEF	LANGUAGE	PILL	THREES
COLORS	LARISSA	PLANES	TWELVES
DECEMBER	LIE	POWER	TWINS
EIGHTS	LILY	RECEIVER	WAR

The Giver Crossword 1

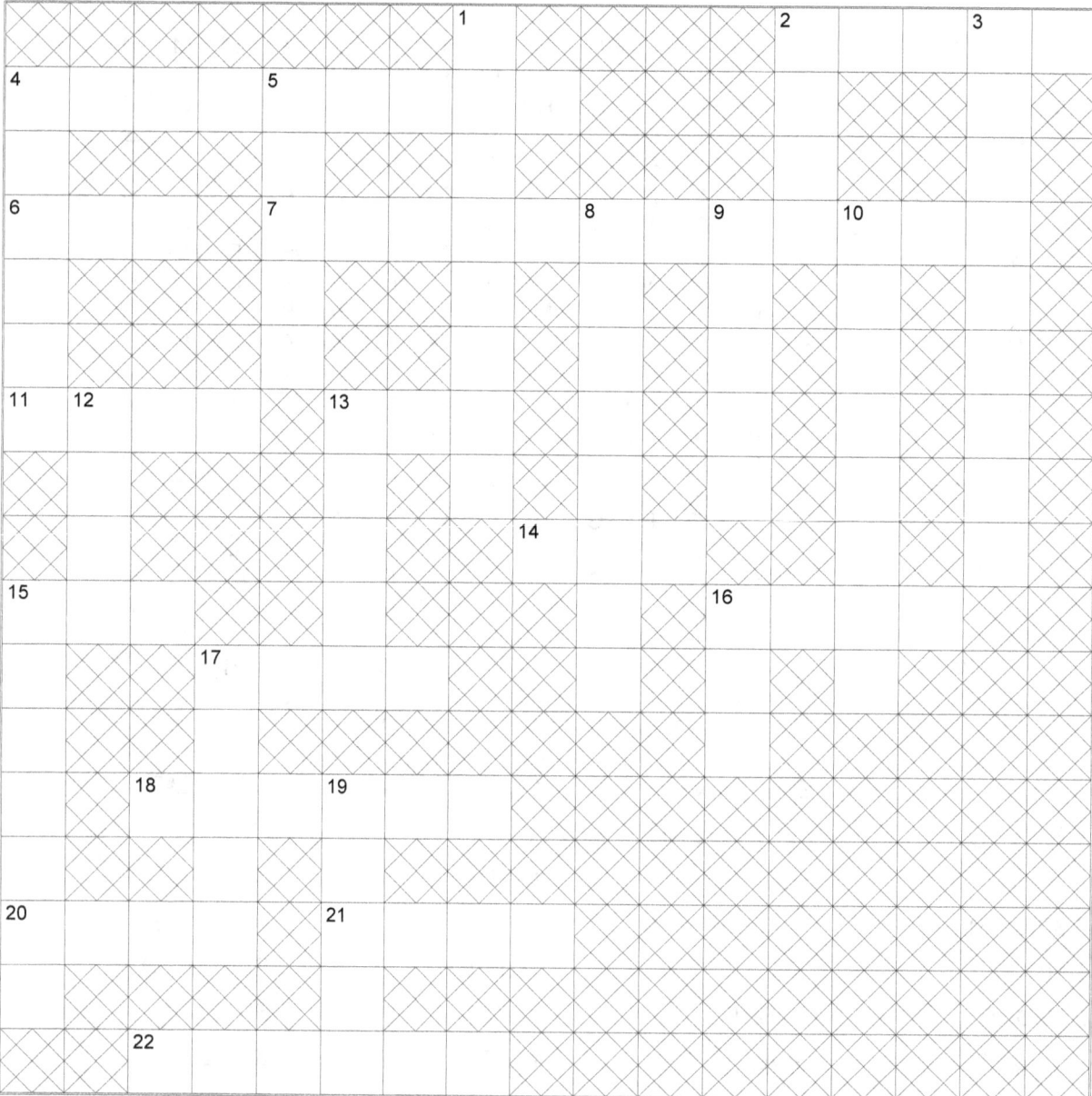

Across
2. The Receiver did not have this
4. Fiona's assignment was ___ of the Old
6. Jonas, as Receiver, could do this
7. Mother's was higher than Father's
11. Jonas found one at the top of the hill
13. Didn't matter after Ceremony of Twelve
14. Jonas recognized when the children played it
15. The color Jonas saw
16. They got names and parents
17. Gabe thought it was a plane
18. She was intelligent
20. They had their long hair cut off
21. The people had never known this
22. Jonas was able to see ___

Down
1. Month of the Ceremony
2. Jonas's and Gabe's eyes looked this way
3. Outside the Community
4. The people could not see them
5. Father released the smaller of them
8. It was to be precise
9. Transferred the memories to Jonas
10. Jonas's number
12. Jonas asked his parents if they felt this for him
13. Had trouble with language
15. Has a release ceremony in House of Old
16. Fiona worked in the House of the ___
17. The Receiver had many in his dwelling
19. Gabe's comfort object

The Giver Crossword 1 Answer Key

							1 D			2 P	O	W	3 E	R
4 C	A	R	E	5 T	A	K	E	R		A			L	
O				W			C			L			S	
6 L	I	E		7 I	N	T	E	8 L	9 I	G	10 E	N	C	E
O				N			M	A	N		I		N		W
R				S			B	N		V		N		H
11 S	12 L	E	D		13 A	G	E		G	E	E	T	E	E
	O				S		R		U	R	T	R
	V				H			14 W	A	R	E	E
15 R	E	D			E				G		16 O	N	E	S
O			17 B	I	R	D			E	L	N
B			O						D
E			18 M	O	T	19 H	E	R
R			K			I
20 T	E	N	S		21 P	A	I	N
O					P
		22 B	E	Y	O	N	D

Across

2. The Receiver did not have this
4. Fiona's assignment was ___ of the Old
6. Jonas, as Receiver, could do this
7. Mother's was higher than Father's
11. Jonas found one at the top of the hill
13. Didn't matter after Ceremony of Twelve
14. Jonas recognized when the children played it
15. The color Jonas saw
16. They got names and parents
17. Gabe thought it was a plane
18. She was intelligent
20. They had their long hair cut off
21. The people had never known this
22. Jonas was able to see ___

Down

1. Month of the Ceremony
2. Jonas's and Gabe's eyes looked this way
3. Outside the Community
4. The people could not see them
5. Father released the smaller of them
8. It was to be precise
9. Transferred the memories to Jonas
10. Jonas's number
12. Jonas asked his parents if they felt this for him
13. Had trouble with language
15. Has a release ceremony in House of Old
16. Fiona worked in the House of the ___
17. The Receiver had many in his dwelling
19. Gabe's comfort object

The Giver Crossword 2

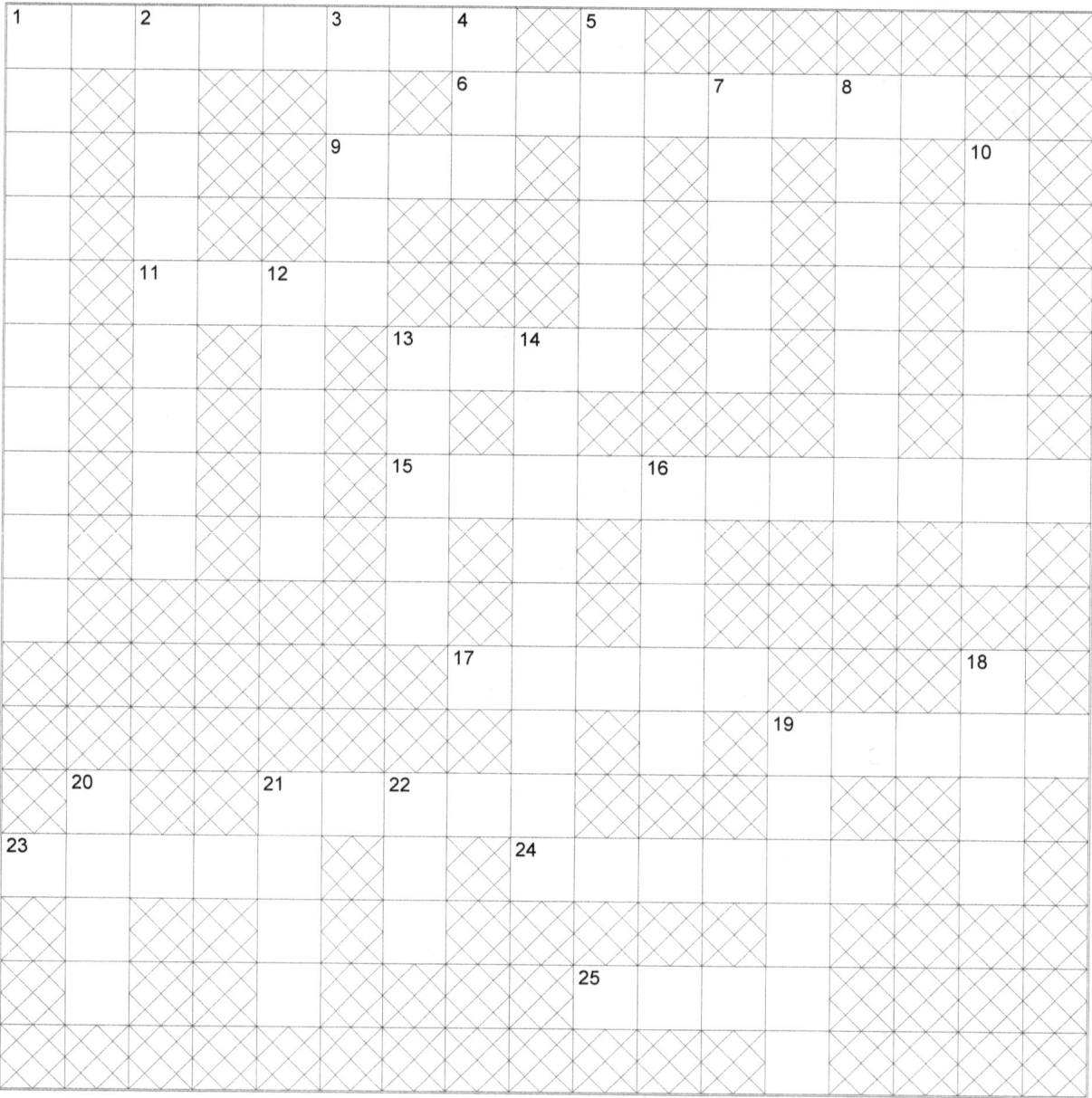

Across
1. Month of the Ceremony
6. Lily's comfort object
9. Fiona worked in the House of the ___
11. They had their long hair cut off
13. Jonas found one at the top of the hill
15. The Elders chose these for the Twelves
17. Announced the assignments: ___ Elder
19. Jonas heard it coming from the bottom of the hill
21. The Receiver did not have this
23. Jonas dreamed about her
24. Had jackets with small buttons and pockets
25. Jonas asked his parents if they felt this for him

Down
1. This wand was a punishment tool for small children
2. Fiona's assignment was ___ of the Old
3. The Receiver had many in his dwelling
4. The color Jonas saw
5. Jonas was able to see ___
7. Gabe's comfort object
8. Jonas's number
10. Has a release ceremony in House of Old
12. They got their bicycles
13. Asher confused it with snack
14. Outside the Community
16. Transferred the memories to Jonas
18. Gabe thought it was a plane
19. She was intelligent
20. Jonas stopped taking his
21. The people had never known this
22. Jonas recognized when the children played it

The Giver Crossword 2 Answer Key

	1 D	2 C	E	M	3 B	E	R		5 B				
	I		A		O		6 E	L	E	7 P	H	8 A	N	T
	S		R		9 O	L	D		Y		I		I		10 R
	C		E		K				O		P		N		O
	I		11 T	12 E	N	S			N		P		E		B
	P		A		I		13 S	14 L	E	D		O		T		E
	L		K		N		M		L					E		R
	I		E		E		15 A	S	S	16 I	G	N	M	E	N	T	S
	N		R		S		C		E		I				N		O
	E						K		W		V						
							17 C	H	I	E	F				18 B
									E		R		19 M	U	S	I	C
		20 P		21 P	O	22 W	E	R				O		R
	23 F	I	O	N	A		A		24 E	I	G	H	T	S		D
		L			I		R					H		
		L			N				25 L	O	V	E		
												R		

Across
1. Month of the Ceremony
6. Lily's comfort object
9. Fiona worked in the House of the ___
11. They had their long hair cut off
13. Jonas found one at the top of the hill
15. The Elders chose these for the Twelves
17. Announced the assignments: ___ Elder
19. Jonas heard it coming from the bottom of the hill
21. The Receiver did not have this
23. Jonas dreamed about her
24. Had jackets with small buttons and pockets
25. Jonas asked his parents if they felt this for him

Down
1. This wand was a punishment tool for small children
2. Fiona's assignment was ___ of the Old
3. The Receiver had many in his dwelling
4. The color Jonas saw
5. Jonas was able to see ___
7. Gabe's comfort object
8. Jonas's number
10. Has a release ceremony in House of Old
12. They got their bicycles
13. Asher confused it with snack
14. Outside the Community
16. Transferred the memories to Jonas
18. Gabe thought it was a plane
19. She was intelligent
20. Jonas stopped taking his
21. The people had never known this
22. Jonas recognized when the children played it

The Giver Crossword 3

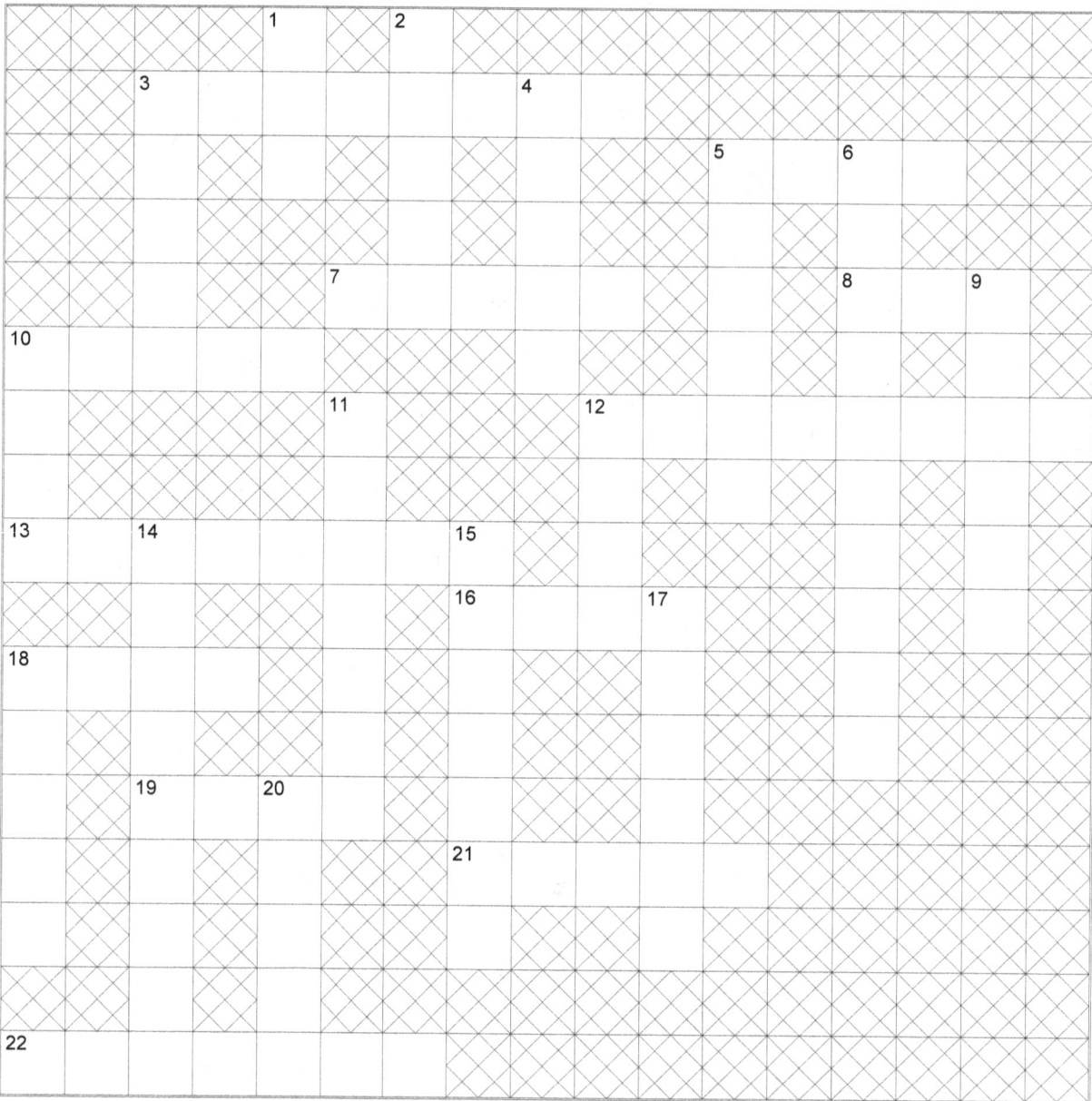

Across
3. Family shared them after dinner
5. Jackets of Fours, Fives & Sixes buttoned down the ___
7. The Receiver did not have this
8. Jonas, as Receiver, could do this
10. Asher confused it with snack
12. It was to be precise
13. Month of the Ceremony
16. They got names and parents
18. Gabe thought it was a plane
19. They had their long hair cut off
21. Father released the smaller of them
22. Described Roberto's ceremony

Down
1. The color Jonas saw
2. Gabe's comfort object
3. Jonas dreamed about her
4. Transferred the memories to Jonas
5. Jonas was able to see ___
6. Male Elevens' pants had a pocket for one
9. Had jackets with small buttons and pockets
10. Jonas found one at the top of the hill
11. Lily didn't like hair ___
12. Jonas asked his parents if they felt this for him
14. Fiona's assignment was ___ of the Old
15. Has a release ceremony in House of Old
17. Their jackets buttoned in front
18. The Receiver had many in his dwelling
20. They got their bicycles

The Giver Crossword 3 Answer Key

Across
3. Family shared them after dinner
5. Jackets of Fours, Fives & Sixes buttoned down the ___
7. The Receiver did not have this
8. Jonas, as Receiver, could do this
10. Asher confused it with snack
12. It was to be precise
13. Month of the Ceremony
16. They got names and parents
18. Gabe thought it was a plane
19. They had their long hair cut off
21. Father released the smaller of them
22. Described Roberto's ceremony

Down
1. The color Jonas saw
2. Gabe's comfort object
3. Jonas dreamed about her
4. Transferred the memories to Jonas
5. Jonas was able to see ___
6. Male Elevens' pants had a pocket for one
9. Had jackets with small buttons and pockets
10. Jonas found one at the top of the hill
11. Lily didn't like hair ___
12. Jonas asked his parents if they felt this for him
14. Fiona's assignment was ___ of the Old
15. Has a release ceremony in House of Old
17. Their jackets buttoned in front
18. The Receiver had many in his dwelling
20. They got their bicycles

The Giver Crossword 4

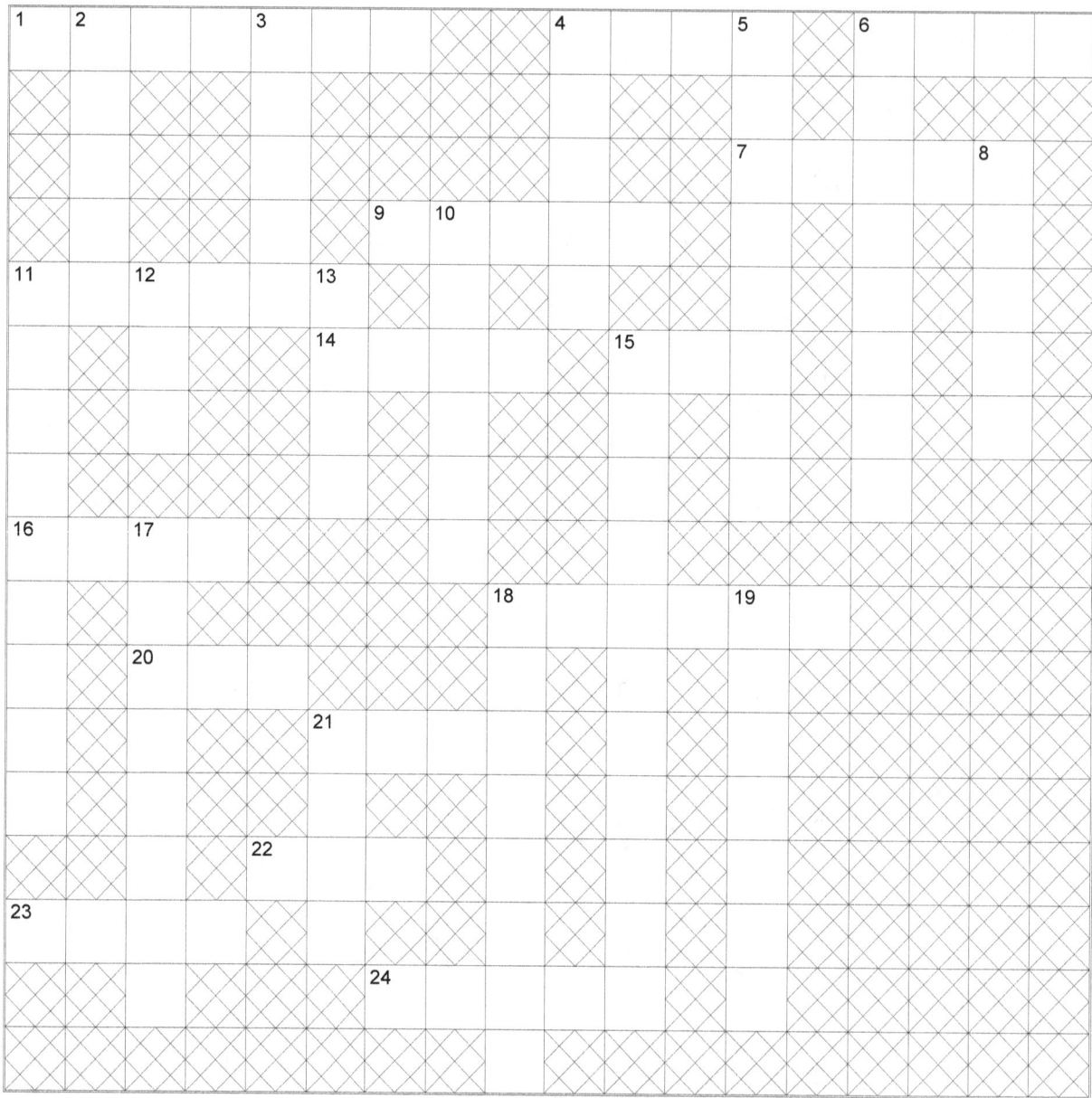

Across
1. What happened to the apple
4. The people had never known this
6. Wanted to be a birthmother
7. They got their bicycles
9. Had trouble with language
11. The people could not see them
14. Jonas asked his parents if they felt this for him
15. Didn't matter after Ceremony of Twelve
16. They had their long hair cut off
18. Had jackets with small buttons and pockets
20. The color Jonas saw
21. Jonas's and Gabe's eyes looked this way
22. Fiona worked in the House of the ___
23. They got names and parents
24. Became the new Receiver of Memory

Down
2. Gabe's comfort object
3. Transferred the memories to Jonas
4. The Receiver did not have this
5. Jonas's number
6. It was to be precise
8. Asher confused it with snack
10. Their jackets buttoned in front
11. Fiona's assignment was ___ of the Old
12. Jonas, as Receiver, could do this
13. Jonas found one at the top of the hill
15. The Elders chose these for the Twelves
17. Father's job
18. Lily's comfort object
19. Got their adult Assignments
21. Jonas stopped taking his

The Giver Crossword 4 Answer Key

	1 C	2 H	A	3 N	G	E	D		4 P	A	5 I	N		6 L	I	L	Y
		I		I					O		I			A			
		P		V					W		7 N	I	N	E	S	8 S	
		P		E		9 A	10 S	H	E	R	E			G		M	
11 C	O	12 L	O	13 R	S		E		R		15 T			U		A	
A		I		14 L	O	V	E		A	G	E			A		C	
R		E		E			E		S		E			G		K	
E				D			N		S		N			E			
16 T	17 E	N	S				S		I								
A	U					18 E	I	G	H	19 T	S					
K	20 R	E	D			L			N	W						
E	T			21 P	A	L	E		M	E						
R	U			I		P			E	L						
	R	22 O	L	D		H			N	V						
23 O	N	E	S		L		A		T	E						
	R			24 J	O	N	A	S	S							
				T												

Across
1. What happened to the apple
4. The people had never known this
6. Wanted to be a birthmother
7. They got their bicycles
9. Had trouble with language
11. The people could not see them
14. Jonas asked his parents if they felt this for him
15. Didn't matter after Ceremony of Twelve
16. They had their long hair cut off
18. Had jackets with small buttons and pockets
20. The color Jonas saw
21. Jonas's and Gabe's eyes looked this way
22. Fiona worked in the House of the ___
23. They got names and parents
24. Became the new Receiver of Memory

Down
2. Gabe's comfort object
3. Transferred the memories to Jonas
4. The Receiver did not have this
5. Jonas's number
6. It was to be precise
8. Asher confused it with snack
10. Their jackets buttoned in front
11. Fiona's assignment was ___ of the Old
12. Jonas, as Receiver, could do this
13. Jonas found one at the top of the hill
15. The Elders chose these for the Twelves
17. Father's job
18. Lily's comfort object
19. Got their adult Assignments
21. Jonas stopped taking his

The Giver

LIE	ASSIGNMENTS	BEYOND	DISPOSITION	PLANES
DISCIPLINE	MOTHER	DECEMBER	ANIMALS	BIRTHMOTHER
CHANGED	SEVENS	FREE SPACE	SAMENESS	HIPPO
ROSEMARY	WAR	PAIN	ELEPHANT	ROBERTO
FEELINGS	BACK	COLORS	FIONA	ASHER

The Giver

TENS	RIBBONS	ONES	SAILING	STIRRINGS
MATURITY	LILY	TWINS	RECREATION	ELSEWHERE
GRANDPARENTS	PILL	FREE SPACE	INTELLIGENCE	BIRD
INDEPENDENCE	TWELVES	JONAS	LANGUAGE	THREES
CHIEF	BICYCLE	POWER	GIVER	MUSIC

The Giver

APPLE	PILL	NURTURER	ELEPHANT	MOTHER
NAMING	CHIEF	FEELINGS	PAIN	ONES
GABRIEL	ELSEWHERE	FREE SPACE	RELEASE	FEMALE
RECREATION	LANGUAGE	LILY	MEMORIES	RED
ASHER	INDEPENDENCE	SEVENS	BICYCLE	POWER

The Giver

JONAS	MATURITY	BOOKS	THREES	NINETEEN
CALCULATOR	SAILING	BIRD	NINES	CHANGED
ANIMALS	DECEMBER	FREE SPACE	TWELVES	LOVE
EIGHTS	GIVER	OLD	SMACK	MUSIC
ASSIGNMENTS	TENS	FIONA	TWINS	AGE

The Giver

ROSEMARY	SMACK	PILL	ASSIGNMENTS	PAIN
CALCULATOR	TENS	BOOKS	NINES	GIVER
SAILING	MALE	FREE SPACE	MATURITY	HONOR
CHIEF	STIRRINGS	RECREATION	FIONA	LANGUAGE
NAMING	ONES	JONAS	FEELINGS	THREES

The Giver

DECEMBER	TWELVES	NINETEEN	EIGHTS	APPLE
INDEPENDENCE	JUSTICE	OLD	LILY	ROBERTO
SAMENESS	SEVENS	FREE SPACE	TWINS	BACK
PALE	ASHER	POWER	BIRTHMOTHER	RECEIVER
RED	LARISSA	FEMALE	SLED	GRANDPARENTS

The Giver

MEMORIES	ELEPHANT	APPLE	ELSEWHERE	RED
ONES	CALCULATOR	COLORS	DISCIPLINE	BICYCLE
TENS	RECREATION	FREE SPACE	FIONA	LIE
BACK	ASSIGNMENTS	TWELVES	AGE	MATURITY
CHIEF	INTELLIGENCE	PALE	DECEMBER	SMACK

The Giver

MALE	EIGHTS	GABRIEL	WAR	DISPOSITION
RIBBONS	ROSEMARY	HIPPO	NAMING	INDEPENDENCE
GIVER	LARISSA	FREE SPACE	MUSIC	LILY
SEVENS	JUSTICE	SLED	STIRRINGS	JONAS
RELEASE	CARETAKER	RECEIVER	TWINS	CHANGED

The Giver

PAIN	CHIEF	BACK	DISPOSITION	PALE
BOOKS	BIRTHMOTHER	ELEPHANT	APPLE	NINETEEN
PILL	TWINS	FREE SPACE	SLED	GIVER
ROSEMARY	MATURITY	RED	ANIMALS	FIONA
BIRD	OLD	HONOR	ROBERTO	STIRRINGS

The Giver

LANGUAGE	FEMALE	RIBBONS	NINES	ASSIGNMENTS
EIGHTS	CARETAKER	CALCULATOR	AGE	RECREATION
GRANDPARENTS	LILY	FREE SPACE	MALE	RECEIVER
LOVE	HIPPO	ONES	TWELVES	MUSIC
MEMORIES	WAR	BICYCLE	COLORS	SMACK

The Giver

ELSEWHERE	WAR	NURTURER	BIRTHMOTHER	INTELLIGENCE
JONAS	HIPPO	TWINS	NINETEEN	BOOKS
CHIEF	HONOR	FREE SPACE	DECEMBER	STIRRINGS
SLED	PAIN	SAILING	SAMENESS	GIVER
APPLE	RECREATION	NAMING	GRANDPARENTS	SMACK

The Giver

MATURITY	RIBBONS	FEELINGS	CALCULATOR	LIE
LILY	CARETAKER	AGE	BICYCLE	ROSEMARY
THREES	SEVENS	FREE SPACE	DISCIPLINE	LARISSA
COLORS	ELEPHANT	RED	PLANES	RECEIVER
MEMORIES	GABRIEL	DISPOSITION	LOVE	RELEASE

The Giver

TENS	DECEMBER	FIONA	ELEPHANT	SMACK
SAILING	WAR	NINES	HIPPO	HONOR
CALCULATOR	ROBERTO	FREE SPACE	MEMORIES	DISCIPLINE
BICYCLE	EIGHTS	RECEIVER	PALE	LOVE
INDEPENDENCE	LIE	MALE	RELEASE	JONAS

The Giver

NURTURER	GABRIEL	SAMENESS	MATURITY	OLD
CHIEF	BIRD	MUSIC	CARETAKER	PLANES
MOTHER	RECREATION	FREE SPACE	GRANDPARENTS	SEVENS
APPLE	CHANGED	ANIMALS	BOOKS	STIRRINGS
AGE	PAIN	BIRTHMOTHER	NINETEEN	FEELINGS

The Giver

BIRTHMOTHER	NAMING	SAILING	MATURITY	BICYCLE
ANIMALS	RECEIVER	RED	PILL	NURTURER
JUSTICE	WAR	FREE SPACE	CALCULATOR	ROSEMARY
COLORS	BOOKS	AGE	DISCIPLINE	DISPOSITION
EIGHTS	ROBERTO	MOTHER	RIBBONS	GABRIEL

The Giver

DECEMBER	MEMORIES	SLED	MALE	CARETAKER
FIONA	CHANGED	HIPPO	LIE	LARISSA
SMACK	LILY	FREE SPACE	RELEASE	BACK
STIRRINGS	NINETEEN	TWINS	ASSIGNMENTS	APPLE
JONAS	LANGUAGE	TWELVES	BIRD	INDEPENDENCE

The Giver

EIGHTS	ELEPHANT	ASHER	PILL	ASSIGNMENTS
MALE	NINES	NINETEEN	OLD	GABRIEL
RECREATION	PALE	FREE SPACE	LANGUAGE	ROSEMARY
LIE	BOOKS	LILY	INDEPENDENCE	BIRD
POWER	APPLE	LOVE	SAILING	ANIMALS

The Giver

THREES	BICYCLE	GIVER	HONOR	CHIEF
FIONA	PLANES	JONAS	RECEIVER	TENS
INTELLIGENCE	FEMALE	FREE SPACE	JUSTICE	MOTHER
RELEASE	DISCIPLINE	TWELVES	COLORS	NURTURER
SEVENS	NAMING	SMACK	HIPPO	MUSIC

The Giver

ROBERTO	LARISSA	FIONA	ASHER	GABRIEL
CARETAKER	SAILING	JONAS	RED	MEMORIES
MATURITY	CHIEF	FREE SPACE	GRANDPARENTS	DISPOSITION
ELSEWHERE	GIVER	NURTURER	CALCULATOR	LANGUAGE
DECEMBER	SMACK	MOTHER	COLORS	LIE

The Giver

FEMALE	PILL	POWER	LOVE	SAMENESS
HIPPO	APPLE	CHANGED	JUSTICE	HONOR
INTELLIGENCE	ELEPHANT	FREE SPACE	BIRTHMOTHER	NINETEEN
RIBBONS	TWELVES	ONES	OLD	RECREATION
BACK	TENS	ASSIGNMENTS	RELEASE	INDEPENDENCE

The Giver

NINES	FEMALE	GIVER	BEYOND	STIRRINGS
SAILING	WAR	LILY	SAMENESS	THREES
RELEASE	ASHER	FREE SPACE	CHIEF	BIRD
APPLE	INDEPENDENCE	ASSIGNMENTS	EIGHTS	HIPPO
HONOR	TENS	BIRTHMOTHER	AGE	PAIN

The Giver

ROSEMARY	FEELINGS	LOVE	MEMORIES	JONAS
JUSTICE	ELSEWHERE	ANIMALS	RECREATION	FIONA
INTELLIGENCE	ROBERTO	FREE SPACE	CARETAKER	NURTURER
CALCULATOR	RECEIVER	LARISSA	TWINS	COLORS
MALE	PALE	TWELVES	ELEPHANT	NAMING

The Giver

MATURITY	AGE	GABRIEL	ANIMALS	LOVE
TWELVES	NURTURER	NAMING	APPLE	RECREATION
DISPOSITION	POWER	FREE SPACE	BIRD	BOOKS
ROBERTO	DECEMBER	TWINS	ONES	ASHER
COLORS	SAMENESS	PALE	BIRTHMOTHER	THREES

The Giver

DISCIPLINE	MOTHER	PILL	JUSTICE	SAILING
NINETEEN	MALE	BEYOND	TENS	ELSEWHERE
GIVER	SMACK	FREE SPACE	GRANDPARENTS	FEMALE
RIBBONS	MUSIC	ELEPHANT	JONAS	SEVENS
BACK	FIONA	CARETAKER	PAIN	CALCULATOR

The Giver

NAMING	BICYCLE	FEELINGS	ROSEMARY	PILL
SAILING	BOOKS	MOTHER	MALE	MUSIC
RECEIVER	OLD	FREE SPACE	PALE	BEYOND
ASSIGNMENTS	DECEMBER	NINES	GIVER	CARETAKER
BIRD	RECREATION	RED	INTELLIGENCE	BIRTHMOTHER

The Giver

RELEASE	CHIEF	ROBERTO	THREES	DISPOSITION
ONES	CALCULATOR	LARISSA	BACK	APPLE
HONOR	PAIN	FREE SPACE	FEMALE	SMACK
SAMENESS	MEMORIES	TWELVES	INDEPENDENCE	FIONA
POWER	GRANDPARENTS	GABRIEL	JONAS	SLED

The Giver

FEELINGS	LILY	CALCULATOR	FEMALE	WAR
BIRTHMOTHER	PALE	BIRD	ELEPHANT	CARETAKER
STIRRINGS	ASHER	FREE SPACE	TENS	INTELLIGENCE
SEVENS	PLANES	RIBBONS	LARISSA	NURTURER
DECEMBER	EIGHTS	GRANDPARENTS	HIPPO	POWER

The Giver

SLED	FIONA	BACK	LANGUAGE	NINETEEN
GABRIEL	LOVE	AGE	BOOKS	PAIN
ASSIGNMENTS	TWINS	FREE SPACE	ROSEMARY	GIVER
MEMORIES	COLORS	RED	RELEASE	NINES
BICYCLE	THREES	MOTHER	PILL	ANIMALS

The Giver

DECEMBER	ASSIGNMENTS	PALE	INTELLIGENCE	DISPOSITION
NURTURER	RELEASE	RECREATION	COLORS	POWER
FEELINGS	PILL	FREE SPACE	TWELVES	BOOKS
ROSEMARY	MUSIC	DISCIPLINE	JONAS	PLANES
FIONA	AGE	HIPPO	MEMORIES	ELSEWHERE

The Giver

THREES	MOTHER	TWINS	CHANGED	SAILING
SEVENS	CALCULATOR	ROBERTO	MATURITY	TENS
EIGHTS	BIRD	FREE SPACE	ONES	RED
JUSTICE	BEYOND	ASHER	OLD	LIE
APPLE	RECEIVER	ELEPHANT	SLED	NINETEEN

The Giver

FEMALE	ASHER	SMACK	JONAS	HIPPO
WAR	MUSIC	RELEASE	ROSEMARY	LILY
ASSIGNMENTS	FIONA	FREE SPACE	JUSTICE	LARISSA
TWELVES	BIRTHMOTHER	CHANGED	RECREATION	ROBERTO
EIGHTS	BOOKS	ELEPHANT	TWINS	MEMORIES

The Giver

DISPOSITION	CALCULATOR	CARETAKER	THREES	SAILING
INTELLIGENCE	RECEIVER	CHIEF	PILL	PALE
NINETEEN	PLANES	FREE SPACE	ONES	FEELINGS
SLED	GRANDPARENTS	DISCIPLINE	POWER	SAMENESS
PAIN	STIRRINGS	ELSEWHERE	HONOR	BICYCLE

Giver Vocabulary Word List

No.	Word	Clue/Definition
1.	ACQUISITION	Purchase
2.	ADMONITION	A reminder of a forgotten task or duty
3.	ANGUISH	Distress; suffering
4.	APPARENT	Visible; easily seen
5.	APPREHENSIVE	Fearful; anxious
6.	APTITUDE	Talent
7.	ASSUAGE	To relieve
8.	BENIGN	Harmless
9.	CAPACITY	Ability to hold
10.	CHAOS	Disorderly confusion
11.	CHASTISEMENT	Punishment
12.	CONCLUSION	The end
13.	CONSPICUOUS	Noticeable
14.	CONTORTED	Twisted; disfigured
15.	CRESCENDO	Gradual increase in volume
16.	CRINGED	Shrank back in fear
17.	DAZED	Stunned; bewildered
18.	DEJECTED	Depressed
19.	DESIGNATED	Indicated; pointed out
20.	DIMINISH	Decrease
21.	DISPOSITION	Personality
22.	DISTRAUGHT	Very upset; agitated
23.	ECSTATIC	Overjoyed
24.	EFFICIENT	Done with a minimum of waste
25.	EMPHATICALLY	Forcefully
26.	ENHANCE	Improve
27.	EXCRUCIATING	Agonizing
28.	EXEMPTED	Excluded from obligation
29.	EXHILARATE	Cause to feel energetic
30.	EXQUISITE	Lovely
31.	EXUBERANT	High-spirited
32.	FRIGID	Very cold
33.	FUGITIVES	People running away
34.	GRAVELY	Requiring serious thought
35.	IMPEDED	Got in the way of progress
36.	INFRINGED	Intruded
37.	INVIGORATING	Refreshing; stimulating
38.	METICULOUSLY	Extremely concerned with details
39.	MURKY	Dark; muddy; not clear
40.	NURTURING	Helping to grow or develop
41.	OBSOLETE	No longer in use
42.	OMINOUS	Threatening
43.	OPTIMISTIC	Hopeful; expecting the best outcome
44.	PALPABLE	Easily perceived; obvious
45.	PERCEIVE	Become aware of through the senses
46.	PERMEATED	Spread or flowing throughout
47.	PETULANTLY	In an ill-tempered way
48.	PLACIDLY	Peacefully
49.	PRECISE	Exact
50.	PRIMLY	In a proper manner
51.	PROHIBITED	Forbidden

Giver Vocabulary Word List Continued

No.	Word	Clue/Definition
52.	RASPING	With a harsh, grating sound
53.	REMORSE	Regret
54.	REPRIEVE	Pardon
55.	SERENE	Calm
56.	SPONTANEOUSLY	Unrehearsed
57.	SUBTLE	Indirect; faint
58.	SUCCESSOR	One who comes next
59.	SURGED	Increased suddenly
60.	TABULATED	Recorded and filed
61.	TENTATIVELY	Uncertainly; with hesitation
62.	THRONG	Crowd
63.	TORRENT	Heavy downpour
64.	TRANSGRESSIONS	Violations of laws or rules
65.	UNANIMOUS	In complete agreement
66.	VAGUE	Indefinite
67.	VIGILANT	Alert; watchful
68.	WRETCHED	Miserable

The Giver Vocabulary Fill In The Blank 1

_____ 1. Done with a minimum of waste
_____ 2. Increased suddenly
_____ 3. Indicated; pointed out
_____ 4. Refreshing; stimulating
_____ 5. One who comes next
_____ 6. Dark; muddy; not clear
_____ 7. Fearful; anxious
_____ 8. Lovely
_____ 9. To relieve
_____ 10. Visible; easily seen
_____ 11. Stunned; bewildered
_____ 12. Depressed
_____ 13. Requiring serious thought
_____ 14. Indefinite
_____ 15. Alert; watchful
_____ 16. No longer in use
_____ 17. Overjoyed
_____ 18. In an ill-tempered way
_____ 19. With a harsh, grating sound
_____ 20. In complete agreement

The Giver Vocabulary Fill In The Blank 1 Answer Key

EFFICIENT	1. Done with a minimum of waste
SURGED	2. Increased suddenly
DESIGNATED	3. Indicated; pointed out
INVIGORATING	4. Refreshing; stimulating
SUCCESSOR	5. One who comes next
MURKY	6. Dark; muddy; not clear
APPREHENSIVE	7. Fearful; anxious
EXQUISITE	8. Lovely
ASSUAGE	9. To relieve
APPARENT	10. Visible; easily seen
DAZED	11. Stunned; bewildered
DEJECTED	12. Depressed
GRAVELY	13. Requiring serious thought
VAGUE	14. Indefinite
VIGILANT	15. Alert; watchful
OBSOLETE	16. No longer in use
ECSTATIC	17. Overjoyed
PETULANTLY	18. In an ill-tempered way
RASPING	19. With a harsh, grating sound
UNANIMOUS	20. In complete agreement

Copyrighted

The Giver Vocabulary Fill in The Blank 2

_____ 1. Intruded

_____ 2. Spread or flowing throughout

_____ 3. Become aware of through the senses

_____ 4. Shrank back in fear

_____ 5. Done with a minimum of waste

_____ 6. The end

_____ 7. Exact

_____ 8. Twisted; disfigured

_____ 9. Uncertainly; with hesitation

_____ 10. Noticeable

_____ 11. Improve

_____ 12. Calm

_____ 13. High-spirited

_____ 14. Recorded and filed

_____ 15. Pardon

_____ 16. Depressed

_____ 17. Punishment

_____ 18. Visible; easily seen

_____ 19. Agonizing

_____ 20. Hopeful; expecting the best outcome

The Giver Vocabulary Fill In The Blank 2 Answer Key

INFRINGED	1. Intruded
PERMEATED	2. Spread or flowing throughout
PERCEIVE	3. Become aware of through the senses
CRINGED	4. Shrank back in fear
EFFICIENT	5. Done with a minimum of waste
CONCLUSION	6. The end
PRECISE	7. Exact
CONTORTED	8. Twisted; disfigured
TENTATIVELY	9. Uncertainly; with hesitation
CONSPICUOUS	10. Noticeable
ENHANCE	11. Improve
SERENE	12. Calm
EXUBERANT	13. High-spirited
TABULATED	14. Recorded and filed
REPRIEVE	15. Pardon
DEJECTED	16. Depressed
CHASTISEMENT	17. Punishment
APPARENT	18. Visible; easily seen
EXCRUCIATING	19. Agonizing
OPTIMISTIC	20. Hopeful; expecting the best outcome

The Giver Vocabulary Fill In The Blank 3

_____ 1. Visible; easily seen

_____ 2. Cause to feel energetic

_____ 3. Hopeful; expecting the best outcome

_____ 4. Intruded

_____ 5. No longer in use

_____ 6. Easily perceived; obvious

_____ 7. Increased suddenly

_____ 8. Ability to hold

_____ 9. Gradual increase in volume

_____ 10. Decrease

_____ 11. Stunned; bewildered

_____ 12. Extremely concerned with details

_____ 13. Dark; muddy; not clear

_____ 14. Regret

_____ 15. With a harsh, grating sound

_____ 16. Distress; suffering

_____ 17. The end

_____ 18. Calm

_____ 19. Disorderly confusion

_____ 20. Very upset; agitated

The Giver Vocabulary Fill In The Blank 3 Answer Key

APPARENT	1. Visible; easily seen
EXHILARATE	2. Cause to feel energetic
OPTIMISTIC	3. Hopeful; expecting the best outcome
INFRINGED	4. Intruded
OBSOLETE	5. No longer in use
PALPABLE	6. Easily perceived; obvious
SURGED	7. Increased suddenly
CAPACITY	8. Ability to hold
CRESCENDO	9. Gradual increase in volume
DIMINISH	10. Decrease
DAZED	11. Stunned; bewildered
METICULOUSLY	12. Extremely concerned with details
MURKY	13. Dark; muddy; not clear
REMORSE	14. Regret
RASPING	15. With a harsh, grating sound
ANGUISH	16. Distress; suffering
CONCLUSION	17. The end
SERENE	18. Calm
CHAOS	19. Disorderly confusion
DISTRAUGHT	20. Very upset; agitated

The Giver Vocabulary Fill In The Blank 4

_____ 1. Twisted; disfigured

_____ 2. No longer in use

_____ 3. Extremely concerned with details

_____ 4. Done with a minimum of waste

_____ 5. Very cold

_____ 6. Ability to hold

_____ 7. Decrease

_____ 8. Improve

_____ 9. High-spirited

_____ 10. Easily perceived; obvious

_____ 11. Helping to grow or develop

_____ 12. Noticeable

_____ 13. Indirect; faint

_____ 14. Alert; watchful

_____ 15. Violations of laws or rules

_____ 16. Forbidden

_____ 17. Fearful; anxious

_____ 18. Personality

_____ 19. Exact

_____ 20. In an ill-tempered way

The Giver Vocabulary Fill In The Blank 4 Answer Key

CONTORTED	1. Twisted; disfigured
OBSOLETE	2. No longer in use
METICULOUSLY	3. Extremely concerned with details
EFFICIENT	4. Done with a minimum of waste
FRIGID	5. Very cold
CAPACITY	6. Ability to hold
DIMINISH	7. Decrease
ENHANCE	8. Improve
EXUBERANT	9. High-spirited
PALPABLE	10. Easily perceived; obvious
NURTURING	11. Helping to grow or develop
CONSPICUOUS	12. Noticeable
SUBTLE	13. Indirect; faint
VIGILANT	14. Alert; watchful
TRANSGRESSIONS	15. Violations of laws or rules
PROHIBITED	16. Forbidden
APPREHENSIVE	17. Fearful; anxious
DISPOSITION	18. Personality
PRECISE	19. Exact
PETULANTLY	20. In an ill-tempered way

The Giver Vocabulary Matching 1

___ 1. APPREHENSIVE   A. Indirect; faint
___ 2. ASSUAGE   B. To relieve
___ 3. DISTRAUGHT   C. Talent
___ 4. CONCLUSION   D. Distress; suffering
___ 5. SERENE   E. Depressed
___ 6. CRESCENDO   F. Personality
___ 7. THRONG   G. Twisted; disfigured
___ 8. APPARENT   H. Forcefully
___ 9. EMPHATICALLY   I. A reminder of a forgotten task or duty
___10. DEJECTED   J. The end
___11. UNANIMOUS   K. Crowd
___12. SURGED   L. Dark; muddy; not clear
___13. ANGUISH   M. Calm
___14. MURKY   N. Recorded and filed
___15. TABULATED   O. In complete agreement
___16. PLACIDLY   P. Lovely
___17. DISPOSITION   Q. Hopeful; expecting the best outcome
___18. CONTORTED   R. Peacefully
___19. CONSPICUOUS   S. Visible; easily seen
___20. EXQUISITE   T. Gradual increase in volume
___21. OPTIMISTIC   U. Fearful; anxious
___22. SUBTLE   V. Regret
___23. ADMONITION   W. Very upset; agitated
___24. APTITUDE   X. Noticeable
___25. REMORSE   Y. Increased suddenly

The Giver Vocabulary Matching 1 Answer Key

U - 1.	APPREHENSIVE	A. Indirect; faint
B - 2.	ASSUAGE	B. To relieve
W - 3.	DISTRAUGHT	C. Talent
J - 4.	CONCLUSION	D. Distress; suffering
M - 5.	SERENE	E. Depressed
T - 6.	CRESCENDO	F. Personality
K - 7.	THRONG	G. Twisted; disfigured
S - 8.	APPARENT	H. Forcefully
H - 9.	EMPHATICALLY	I. A reminder of a forgotten task or duty
E - 10.	DEJECTED	J. The end
O - 11.	UNANIMOUS	K. Crowd
Y - 12.	SURGED	L. Dark; muddy; not clear
D - 13.	ANGUISH	M. Calm
L - 14.	MURKY	N. Recorded and filed
N - 15.	TABULATED	O. In complete agreement
R - 16.	PLACIDLY	P. Lovely
F - 17.	DISPOSITION	Q. Hopeful; expecting the best outcome
G - 18.	CONTORTED	R. Peacefully
X - 19.	CONSPICUOUS	S. Visible; easily seen
P - 20.	EXQUISITE	T. Gradual increase in volume
Q - 21.	OPTIMISTIC	U. Fearful; anxious
A - 22.	SUBTLE	V. Regret
I - 23.	ADMONITION	W. Very upset; agitated
C - 24.	APTITUDE	X. Noticeable
V - 25.	REMORSE	Y. Increased suddenly

The Giver Vocabulary Matching 2

___ 1. DIMINISH   A. Heavy downpour
___ 2. CONTORTED   B. Excluded from obligation
___ 3. TRANSGRESSIONS   C. Crowd
___ 4. DISPOSITION   D. Violations of laws or rules
___ 5. ACQUISITION   E. Indefinite
___ 6. IMPEDED   F. Gradual increase in volume
___ 7. EXHILARATE   G. Distress; suffering
___ 8. CRESCENDO   H. Decrease
___ 9. SERENE   I. No longer in use
___10. UNANIMOUS   J. Agonizing
___11. EFFICIENT   K. Twisted; disfigured
___12. VAGUE   L. Got in the way of progress
___13. REPRIEVE   M. To relieve
___14. PLACIDLY   N. Improve
___15. ASSUAGE   O. Personality
___16. EXEMPTED   P. Calm
___17. EXCRUCIATING   Q. Cause to feel energetic
___18. ENHANCE   R. Peacefully
___19. PETULANTLY   S. Pardon
___20. EXUBERANT   T. Depressed
___21. OBSOLETE   U. Purchase
___22. TORRENT   V. High-spirited
___23. DEJECTED   W. Done with a minimum of waste
___24. ANGUISH   X. In complete agreement
___25. THRONG   Y. In an ill-tempered way

The Giver Vocabulary Matching 2 Answer Key

H - 1.	DIMINISH	A.	Heavy downpour
K - 2.	CONTORTED	B.	Excluded from obligation
D - 3.	TRANSGRESSIONS	C.	Crowd
O - 4.	DISPOSITION	D.	Violations of laws or rules
U - 5.	ACQUISITION	E.	Indefinite
L - 6.	IMPEDED	F.	Gradual increase in volume
Q - 7.	EXHILARATE	G.	Distress; suffering
F - 8.	CRESCENDO	H.	Decrease
P - 9.	SERENE	I.	No longer in use
X - 10.	UNANIMOUS	J.	Agonizing
W - 11.	EFFICIENT	K.	Twisted; disfigured
E - 12.	VAGUE	L.	Got in the way of progress
S - 13.	REPRIEVE	M.	To relieve
R - 14.	PLACIDLY	N.	Improve
M - 15.	ASSUAGE	O.	Personality
B - 16.	EXEMPTED	P.	Calm
J - 17.	EXCRUCIATING	Q.	Cause to feel energetic
N - 18.	ENHANCE	R.	Peacefully
Y - 19.	PETULANTLY	S.	Pardon
V - 20.	EXUBERANT	T.	Depressed
I - 21.	OBSOLETE	U.	Purchase
A - 22.	TORRENT	V.	High-spirited
T - 23.	DEJECTED	W.	Done with a minimum of waste
G - 24.	ANGUISH	X.	In complete agreement
C - 25.	THRONG	Y.	In an ill-tempered way

The Giver Vocabulary Matching 3

___ 1. NURTURING   A. Hopeful; expecting the best outcome
___ 2. ECSTATIC   B. Purchase
___ 3. THRONG   C. Recorded and filed
___ 4. INVIGORATING   D. Stunned; bewildered
___ 5. EXHILARATE   E. Cause to feel energetic
___ 6. ANGUISH   F. Crowd
___ 7. FUGITIVES   G. Miserable
___ 8. EXUBERANT   H. Indirect; faint
___ 9. SERENE   I. Overjoyed
___10. OPTIMISTIC   J. Unrehearsed
___11. METICULOUSLY   K. With a harsh, grating sound
___12. UNANIMOUS   L. Extremely concerned with details
___13. CONTORTED   M. Refreshing; stimulating
___14. WRETCHED   N. Improve
___15. ACQUISITION   O. In complete agreement
___16. APPARENT   P. Alert; watchful
___17. SPONTANEOUSLY   Q. Distress; suffering
___18. TABULATED   R. Calm
___19. EXCRUCIATING   S. Heavy downpour
___20. RASPING   T. Twisted; disfigured
___21. VIGILANT   U. Helping to grow or develop
___22. TORRENT   V. People running away
___23. ENHANCE   W. High-spirited
___24. DAZED   X. Visible; easily seen
___25. SUBTLE   Y. Agonizing

The Giver Vocabulary Matching 3 Answer Key

U - 1. NURTURING	A.	Hopeful; expecting the best outcome
I - 2. ECSTATIC	B.	Purchase
F - 3. THRONG	C.	Recorded and filed
M - 4. INVIGORATING	D.	Stunned; bewildered
E - 5. EXHILARATE	E.	Cause to feel energetic
Q - 6. ANGUISH	F.	Crowd
V - 7. FUGITIVES	G.	Miserable
W - 8. EXUBERANT	H.	Indirect; faint
R - 9. SERENE	I.	Overjoyed
A - 10. OPTIMISTIC	J.	Unrehearsed
L - 11. METICULOUSLY	K.	With a harsh, grating sound
O - 12. UNANIMOUS	L.	Extremely concerned with details
T - 13. CONTORTED	M.	Refreshing; stimulating
G - 14. WRETCHED	N.	Improve
B - 15. ACQUISITION	O.	In complete agreement
X - 16. APPARENT	P.	Alert; watchful
J - 17. SPONTANEOUSLY	Q.	Distress; suffering
C - 18. TABULATED	R.	Calm
Y - 19. EXCRUCIATING	S.	Heavy downpour
K - 20. RASPING	T.	Twisted; disfigured
P - 21. VIGILANT	U.	Helping to grow or develop
S - 22. TORRENT	V.	People running away
N - 23. ENHANCE	W.	High-spirited
D - 24. DAZED	X.	Visible; easily seen
H - 25. SUBTLE	Y.	Agonizing

The Giver Vocabulary Matching 4

___ 1. CHAOS   A. Disorderly confusion
___ 2. WRETCHED   B. No longer in use
___ 3. PLACIDLY   C. With a harsh, grating sound
___ 4. ENHANCE   D. Shrank back in fear
___ 5. VAGUE   E. Gradual increase in volume
___ 6. EMPHATICALLY   F. Unrehearsed
___ 7. SPONTANEOUSLY   G. Excluded from obligation
___ 8. BENIGN   H. Indicated; pointed out
___ 9. SERENE   I. Calm
___10. THRONG   J. Very upset; agitated
___11. CAPACITY   K. Crowd
___12. DAZED   L. Forcefully
___13. CRINGED   M. Harmless
___14. EXHILARATE   N. Ability to hold
___15. DESIGNATED   O. Stunned; bewildered
___16. OBSOLETE   P. Cause to feel energetic
___17. APPARENT   Q. Peacefully
___18. NURTURING   R. The end
___19. EXEMPTED   S. Dark; muddy; not clear
___20. RASPING   T. Hopeful; expecting the best outcome
___21. CRESCENDO   U. Helping to grow or develop
___22. OPTIMISTIC   V. Indefinite
___23. MURKY   W. Miserable
___24. CONCLUSION   X. Visible; easily seen
___25. DISTRAUGHT   Y. Improve

The Giver Vocabulary Matching 4 Answer Key

A - 1. CHAOS	A.	Disorderly confusion
W - 2. WRETCHED	B.	No longer in use
Q - 3. PLACIDLY	C.	With a harsh, grating sound
Y - 4. ENHANCE	D.	Shrank back in fear
V - 5. VAGUE	E.	Gradual increase in volume
L - 6. EMPHATICALLY	F.	Unrehearsed
F - 7. SPONTANEOUSLY	G.	Excluded from obligation
M - 8. BENIGN	H.	Indicated; pointed out
I - 9. SERENE	I.	Calm
K - 10. THRONG	J.	Very upset; agitated
N - 11. CAPACITY	K.	Crowd
O - 12. DAZED	L.	Forcefully
D - 13. CRINGED	M.	Harmless
P - 14. EXHILARATE	N.	Ability to hold
H - 15. DESIGNATED	O.	Stunned; bewildered
B - 16. OBSOLETE	P.	Cause to feel energetic
X - 17. APPARENT	Q.	Peacefully
U - 18. NURTURING	R.	The end
G - 19. EXEMPTED	S.	Dark; muddy; not clear
C - 20. RASPING	T.	Hopeful; expecting the best outcome
E - 21. CRESCENDO	U.	Helping to grow or develop
T - 22. OPTIMISTIC	V.	Indefinite
S - 23. MURKY	W.	Miserable
R - 24. CONCLUSION	X.	Visible; easily seen
J - 25. DISTRAUGHT	Y.	Improve

The Giver Vocabulary Magic Squares 1

Match the definition with the vocabulary word. Put your answers in the magic squares below. When your answers are correct, all columns and rows will add to the same number.

A. OMINOUS
B. SURGED
C. FUGITIVES
D. VIGILANT
E. CHASTISEMENT
F. TORRENT
G. INVIGORATING
H. TABULATED
I. CRESCENDO
J. UNANIMOUS
K. NURTURING
L. EXQUISITE
M. EMPHATICALLY
N. PROHIBITED
O. CRINGED
P. PALPABLE

1. Shrank back in fear
2. In complete agreement
3. Recorded and filed
4. Threatening
5. Alert; watchful
6. Punishment
7. Helping to grow or develop
8. Forbidden
9. Heavy downpour
10. People running away
11. Forcefully
12. Lovely
13. Gradual increase in volume
14. Easily perceived; obvious
15. Increased suddenly
16. Refreshing; stimulating

A=	B=	C=	D=
E=	F=	G=	H=
I=	J=	K=	L=
M=	N=	O=	P=

The Giver Vocabulary Magic Squares 1 Answer Key

Match the definition with the vocabulary word. Put your answers in the magic squares below. When your answers are correct, all columns and rows will add to the same number.

A. OMINOUS
B. SURGED
C. FUGITIVES
D. VIGILANT
E. CHASTISEMENT
F. TORRENT
G. INVIGORATING
H. TABULATED
I. CRESCENDO
J. UNANIMOUS
K. NURTURING
L. EXQUISITE
M. EMPHATICALLY
N. PROHIBITED
O. CRINGED
P. PALPABLE

1. Shrank back in fear
2. In complete agreement
3. Recorded and filed
4. Threatening
5. Alert; watchful
6. Punishment
7. Helping to grow or develop
8. Forbidden
9. Heavy downpour
10. People running away
11. Forcefully
12. Lovely
13. Gradual increase in volume
14. Easily perceived; obvious
15. Increased suddenly
16. Refreshing; stimulating

A=4	B=15	C=10	D=5
E=6	F=9	G=16	H=3
I=13	J=2	K=7	L=12
M=11	N=8	O=1	P=14

The Giver Vocabulary Magic Squares 2

Match the definition with the vocabulary word. Put your answers in the magic squares below. When your answers are correct, all columns and rows will add to the same number.

A. INVIGORATING
B. ASSUAGE
C. DISTRAUGHT
D. CONSPICUOUS
E. NURTURING
F. SUCCESSOR
G. VAGUE
H. CONCLUSION
I. OPTIMISTIC
J. PRIMLY
K. METICULOUSLY
L. DISPOSITION
M. REMORSE
N. ANGUISH
O. EXCRUCIATING
P. FRIGID

1. To relieve
2. Indefinite
3. Extremely concerned with details
4. Distress; suffering
5. Regret
6. Personality
7. The end
8. Refreshing; stimulating
9. Very cold
10. Hopeful; expecting the best outcome
11. Helping to grow or develop
12. Noticeable
13. Very upset; agitated
14. One who comes next
15. In a proper manner
16. Agonizing

A=	B=	C=	D=
E=	F=	G=	H=
I=	J=	K=	L=
M=	N=	O=	P=

The Giver Vocabulary Magic Squares 2 Answer Key

Match the definition with the vocabulary word. Put your answers in the magic squares below. When your answers are correct, all columns and rows will add to the same number.

A. INVIGORATING
B. ASSUAGE
C. DISTRAUGHT
D. CONSPICUOUS
E. NURTURING
F. SUCCESSOR
G. VAGUE
H. CONCLUSION
I. OPTIMISTIC
J. PRIMLY
K. METICULOUSLY
L. DISPOSITION
M. REMORSE
N. ANGUISH
O. EXCRUCIATING
P. FRIGID

1. To relieve
2. Indefinite
3. Extremely concerned with details
4. Distress; suffering
5. Regret
6. Personality
7. The end
8. Refreshing; stimulating
9. Very cold
10. Hopeful; expecting the best outcome
11. Helping to grow or develop
12. Noticeable
13. Very upset; agitated
14. One who comes next
15. In a proper manner
16. Agonizing

A=8	B=1	C=13	D=12
E=11	F=14	G=2	H=7
I=10	J=15	K=3	L=6
M=5	N=4	O=16	P=9

The Giver Vocabulary Magic Squares 3

Match the definition with the vocabulary word. Put your answers in the magic squares below. When your answers are correct, all columns and rows will add to the same number.

A. APPARENT
B. TORRENT
C. SPONTANEOUSLY
D. EXUBERANT
E. EXHILARATE
F. CONCLUSION
G. PERCEIVE
H. CRESCENDO
I. PERMEATED
J. TRANSGRESSIONS
K. ASSUAGE
L. VIGILANT
M. ENHANCE
N. CHAOS
O. ACQUISITION
P. REPRIEVE

1. The end
2. Spread or flowing throughout
3. Purchase
4. High-spirited
5. Improve
6. Heavy downpour
7. Gradual increase in volume
8. To relieve
9. Unrehearsed
10. Pardon
11. Violations of laws or rules
12. Cause to feel energetic
13. Alert; watchful
14. Become aware of through the senses
15. Visible; easily seen
16. Disorderly confusion

A=	B=	C=	D=
E=	F=	G=	H=
I=	J=	K=	L=
M=	N=	O=	P=

The Giver Vocabulary Magic Squares 3 Answer Key

Match the definition with the vocabulary word. Put your answers in the magic squares below. When your answers are correct, all columns and rows will add to the same number.

A. APPARENT
B. TORRENT
C. SPONTANEOUSLY
D. EXUBERANT
E. EXHILARATE
F. CONCLUSION
G. PERCEIVE
H. CRESCENDO
I. PERMEATED
J. TRANSGRESSIONS
K. ASSUAGE
L. VIGILANT
M. ENHANCE
N. CHAOS
O. ACQUISITION
P. REPRIEVE

1. The end
2. Spread or flowing throughout
3. Purchase
4. High-spirited
5. Improve
6. Heavy downpour
7. Gradual increase in volume
8. To relieve
9. Unrehearsed
10. Pardon
11. Violations of laws or rules
12. Cause to feel energetic
13. Alert; watchful
14. Become aware of through the senses
15. Visible; easily seen
16. Disorderly confusion

A=15	B=6	C=9	D=4
E=12	F=1	G=14	H=7
I=2	J=11	K=8	L=13
M=5	N=16	O=3	P=10

The Giver Vocabulary Magic Squares 4

Match the definition with the vocabulary word. Put your answers in the magic squares below. When your answers are correct, all columns and rows will add to the same number.

A. TENTATIVELY
B. DIMINISH
C. CHAOS
D. CRINGED
E. GRAVELY
F. CRESCENDO
G. MURKY
H. CONTORTED
I. FRIGID
J. APPARENT
K. PLACIDLY
L. VIGILANT
M. RASPING
N. METICULOUSLY
O. EXEMPTED
P. REMORSE

1. Twisted; disfigured
2. With a harsh, grating sound
3. Decrease
4. Peacefully
5. Visible; easily seen
6. Disorderly confusion
7. Regret
8. Requiring serious thought
9. Excluded from obligation
10. Gradual increase in volume
11. Very cold
12. Shrank back in fear
13. Uncertainly; with hesitation
14. Alert; watchful
15. Dark; muddy; not clear
16. Extremely concerned with details

A=	B=	C=	D=
E=	F=	G=	H=
I=	J=	K=	L=
M=	N=	O=	P=

The Giver Vocabulary Magic Squares 4 Answer Key

Match the definition with the vocabulary word. Put your answers in the magic squares below. When your answers are correct, all columns and rows will add to the same number.

A. TENTATIVELY
B. DIMINISH
C. CHAOS
D. CRINGED
E. GRAVELY
F. CRESCENDO
G. MURKY
H. CONTORTED
I. FRIGID
J. APPARENT
K. PLACIDLY
L. VIGILANT
M. RASPING
N. METICULOUSLY
O. EXEMPTED
P. REMORSE

1. Twisted; disfigured
2. With a harsh, grating sound
3. Decrease
4. Peacefully
5. Visible; easily seen
6. Disorderly confusion
7. Regret
8. Requiring serious thought
9. Excluded from obligation
10. Gradual increase in volume
11. Very cold
12. Shrank back in fear
13. Uncertainly; with hesitation
14. Alert; watchful
15. Dark; muddy; not clear
16. Extremely concerned with details

A=13	B=3	C=6	D=12
E=8	F=10	G=15	H=1
I=11	J=5	K=4	L=14
M=2	N=16	O=9	P=7

The Giver Vocabulary Word Search 1

```
P E T U L A N T L Y L D I C A L P H E N
Y T H G S E S R O M E R O B G J K T T T
S V S N U K K J R D X N D E T C E J E D
K C I I B Q K O E Z C F F V S L M V Q D
M E U T Y S P Z L Y W B Y O D I Q D K
O T G A L S M Q U Z L Y S W E Q F J E
D I N I E I A S M V M V B V C S R F N S
N S A C Q U I S I T I O N R F I V H Y W
E I C U O O D L S G R Z E S G G A L N F
C U R R N N E M I U P P V I H N L P U M
S Q A C B V T L U E A D D S C A V A R F
E X S X L H A O X R E G U E C T A L T K
R E P E R N E E R Z K O E I V E G P U F
C D I O T G M C A T N Y T P G D U A R Q
H E N K G P R D H I E A W T R C E B I T
N G G Q T D E A M A H D P R A E W L N G
L N D E S W P O V P O P B P E G C E G C
X I D R U N S X M E Z S A E A T R I W W
B R S E R E N E J K L C Z X N R C R S X
C F D E G N I R C J I Y L P O I E H S E
S N Y L E V I T A T N E T T J N G N E P
R I H X D B P X Y R E P R I E V E N T D
```

Ability to hold (8)
Agonizing (12)
Alert; watchful (8)
Become aware of through the senses (8)
Calm (6)
Crowd (6)
Dark; muddy; not clear (5)
Depressed (8)
Disorderly confusion (5)
Distress; suffering (7)
Easily perceived; obvious (8)
Exact (7)
Excluded from obligation (8)
Forcefully (12)
Got in the way of progress (7)
Gradual increase in volume (9)
Harmless (6)
Heavy downpour (7)
Helping to grow or develop (9)
Improve (7)
In a proper manner (6)
In an ill-tempered way (10)
Increased suddenly (6)
Indefinite (5)

Indicated; pointed out (10)
Indirect; faint (6)
Intruded (9)
Lovely (9)
Miserable (8)
No longer in use (8)
One who comes next (9)
Pardon (8)
Peacefully (8)
Purchase (11)
Regret (7)
Requiring serious thought (7)
Shrank back in fear (7)
Spread or flowing throughout (9)
Stunned; bewildered (5)
The end (10)
Threatening (7)
To relieve (7)
Twisted; disfigured (9)
Uncertainly; with hesitation (11)
Very cold (6)
Visible; easily seen (8)
With a harsh, grating sound (7)

The Giver Vocabulary Word Search 1 Answer Key

Ability to hold (8)
Agonizing (12)
Alert; watchful (8)
Become aware of through the senses (8)
Calm (6)
Crowd (6)
Dark; muddy; not clear (5)
Depressed (8)
Disorderly confusion (5)
Distress; suffering (7)
Easily perceived; obvious (8)
Exact (7)
Excluded from obligation (8)
Forcefully (12)
Got in the way of progress (7)
Gradual increase in volume (9)
Harmless (6)
Heavy downpour (7)
Helping to grow or develop (9)
Improve (7)
In a proper manner (6)
In an ill-tempered way (10)
Increased suddenly (6)
Indefinite (5)

Indicated; pointed out (10)
Indirect; faint (6)
Intruded (9)
Lovely (9)
Miserable (8)
No longer in use (8)
One who comes next (9)
Pardon (8)
Peacefully (8)
Purchase (11)
Regret (7)
Requiring serious thought (7)
Shrank back in fear (7)
Spread or flowing throughout (9)
Stunned; bewildered (5)
The end (10)
Threatening (7)
To relieve (7)
Twisted; disfigured (9)
Uncertainly; with hesitation (11)
Very cold (6)
Visible; easily seen (8)
With a harsh, grating sound (7)

The Giver Vocabulary Word Search 2

```
B E N I G N I T A R O G I V N I W Y F B
I A N G U I S H Y P V D T S E T L K R V
A M J L M K Z P P P T T E S V D K R I V
X S P E R M E A T E D I R J I X C U G J
G K S E D Q H P M R M O T C E L S M I K
T C P U D D L P S C M R A U T C V F D C
B O S M A E D A B E Y L W M D I T V P W
T H R O N G D R R I P S U R G E D E R D
E L O R V D E E D V K Q H I P Q F E D M
M M X M E A G N T E T V L L D W T V S V
E L P V I N D T H E S A Y T I C A P A C
L P Y H M N T M N A N I Z B H D B C H H
B Y S G A D O T O T N R G E C V U R W N
A P E L V T A U H N E C D N R B L I D S
P G R F V T I L S P I W E C A D A N I Y
L V E Q I M Y C R C T X H S T T G M K
A V N V L M L I A E Y N I A P Y E E I C
P R E C I S E T E L O S B O I E D D N M
B L Z B Y V V N M T L Q C S N U F C I C
Y X Z K E Q A I R B K Y R M G G S F S F
G N I R U T R U N U D I S T R A U G H T
D A Z E D P G E C S T A T I C V G S J G
```

A reminder of a forgotten task or duty (10)
Ability to hold (8)
Alert; watchful (8)
Become aware of through the senses (8)
Calm (6)
Crowd (6)
Dark; muddy; not clear (5)
Decrease (8)
Depressed (8)
Disorderly confusion (5)
Distress; suffering (7)
Easily perceived; obvious (8)
Exact (7)
Forcefully (12)
Got in the way of progress (7)
Harmless (6)
Heavy downpour (7)
Helping to grow or develop (9)
Improve (7)
In a proper manner (6)
Increased suddenly (6)
Indefinite (5)
Indicated; pointed out (10)
Indirect; faint (6)

Miserable (8)
No longer in use (8)
Overjoyed (8)
Pardon (8)
Peacefully (8)
Recorded and filed (9)
Refreshing; stimulating (12)
Regret (7)
Requiring serious thought (7)
Shrank back in fear (7)
Spread or flowing throughout (9)
Stunned; bewildered (5)
Talent (8)
Threatening (7)
To relieve (7)
Uncertainly; with hesitation (11)
Very cold (6)
Very upset; agitated (10)
Visible; easily seen (8)
With a harsh, grating sound (7)

The Giver Vocabulary Word Search 2 Answer Key

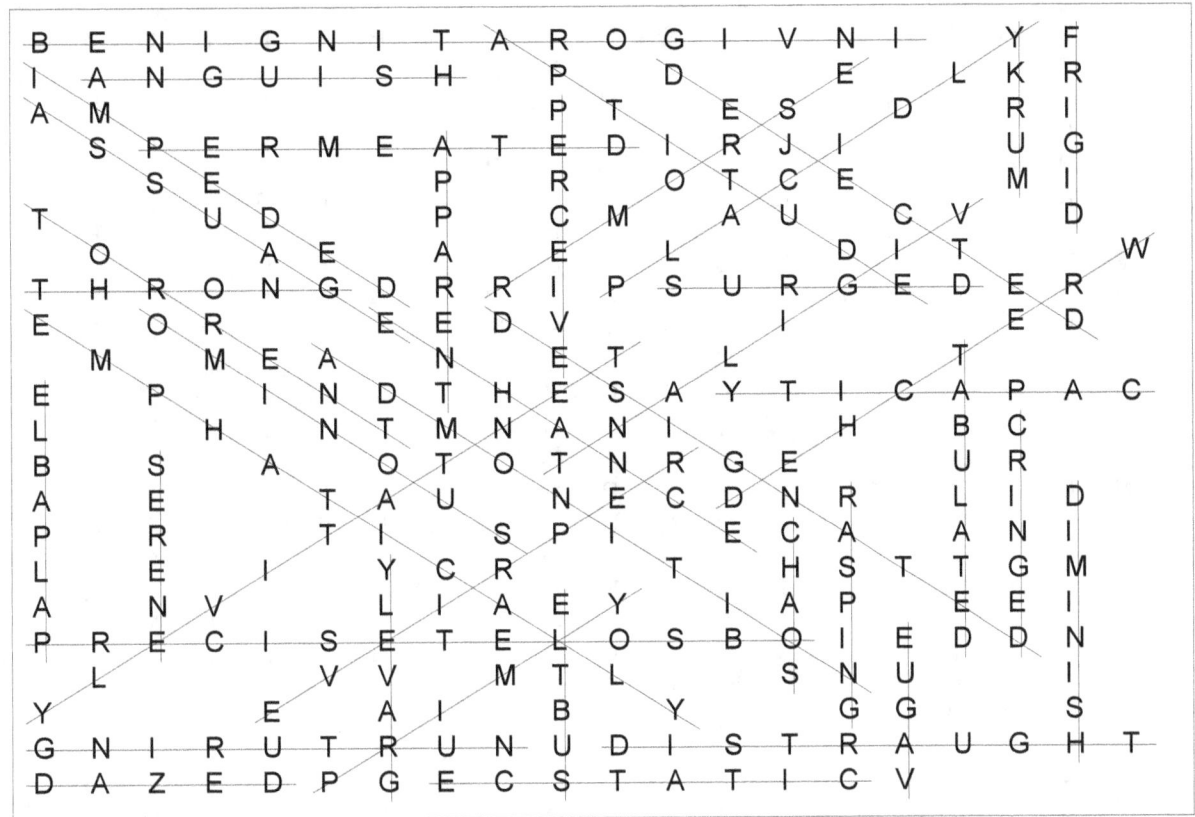

A reminder of a forgotten task or duty (10)
Ability to hold (8)
Alert; watchful (8)
Become aware of through the senses (8)
Calm (6)
Crowd (6)
Dark; muddy; not clear (5)
Decrease (8)
Depressed (8)
Disorderly confusion (5)
Distress; suffering (7)
Easily perceived; obvious (8)
Exact (7)
Forcefully (12)
Got in the way of progress (7)
Harmless (6)
Heavy downpour (7)
Helping to grow or develop (9)
Improve (7)
In a proper manner (6)
Increased suddenly (6)
Indefinite (5)
Indicated; pointed out (10)
Indirect; faint (6)

Miserable (8)
No longer in use (8)
Overjoyed (8)
Pardon (8)
Peacefully (8)
Recorded and filed (9)
Refreshing; stimulating (12)
Regret (7)
Requiring serious thought (7)
Shrank back in fear (7)
Spread or flowing throughout (9)
Stunned; bewildered (5)
Talent (8)
Threatening (7)
To relieve (7)
Uncertainly; with hesitation (11)
Very cold (6)
Very upset; agitated (10)
Visible; easily seen (8)
With a harsh, grating sound (7)

The Giver Vocabulary Word Search 3

```
S U C C E S S O R D S M I M P E D E D Y
Y E C S T A T I C E V E R P E R S T T
A T J L S S S O O J P T R V D H Y I N F
F S H D G J N A N E R I K E B G C C A P
C B S R R T H N S C O C R N A D E L P V
N R P U O V K G P T H U C L P E S R I W
C K E R A N S U I E I L N A Z D U P G F
V V T S I G G I C D B O C A F H O C I N
Q E C N C M E S U V I U D S N F N B V A
D R H U E E L H O P T S Y V Y I I L D F
T A A R X N N Y U L E L P L A Z M M F Y
O S O T H H T D S R D Y T O N G O O P F
R P S U I A O W O I E N J Y S N U S U H
R I X R L N Q B C A A M L D I I E E V S
E N L I A C S A S L P S O T P V T X X D
N G R N R E L B U O U P I R I P X I E G
T P X G A P G T D O L O A T S T Y S O L
W A X T Q E T E D N E I R E E I U F N
R C B S E P R N N H Z G T X E G F R M F
E S R U T N A R E B U X E E N N R G U Y
T T U I L T V F B F E M N A G H T E R H
C Z V B N A G P G B P N T G T S D K Q
H H J O T G T S S T N E I C I F F E Y W
E G P G S L E E E X D V T G F R I G I D
D S H T R R E D D Y J D E G N I R F N I
```

ADMONITION	DESIGNATED	MURKY	SPONTANEOUSLY
ANGUISH	DISPOSITION	NURTURING	SUBTLE
APPARENT	ECSTATIC	OBSOLETE	SUCCESSOR
ASSUAGE	EFFICIENT	OMINOUS	SURGED
BENIGN	ENHANCE	PETULANTLY	TABULATED
CAPACITY	EXEMPTED	PLACIDLY	THRONG
CHAOS	EXHILARATE	PRECISE	TORRENT
CONSPICUOUS	EXUBERANT	PRIMLY	UNANIMOUS
CONTORTED	FRIGID	PROHIBITED	VAGUE
CRESCENDO	FUGITIVES	RASPING	VIGILANT
CRINGED	IMPEDED	REMORSE	WRETCHED
DAZED	INFRINGED	REPRIEVE	
DEJECTED	METICULOUSLY	SERENE	

The Giver Vocabulary Word Search 3 Answer Key

ADMONITION	DESIGNATED	MURKY	SPONTANEOUSLY
ANGUISH	DISPOSITION	NURTURING	SUBTLE
APPARENT	ECSTATIC	OBSOLETE	SUCCESSOR
ASSUAGE	EFFICIENT	OMINOUS	SURGED
BENIGN	ENHANCE	PETULANTLY	TABULATED
CAPACITY	EXEMPTED	PLACIDLY	THRONG
CHAOS	EXHILARATE	PRECISE	TORRENT
CONSPICUOUS	EXUBERANT	PRIMLY	UNANIMOUS
CONTORTED	FRIGID	PROHIBITED	VAGUE
CRESCENDO	FUGITIVES	RASPING	VIGILANT
CRINGED	IMPEDED	REMORSE	WRETCHED
DAZED	INFRINGED	REPRIEVE	
DEJECTED	METICULOUSLY	SERENE	

The Giver Vocabulary Word Search 4

```
I N F R I N G E D P E Y P T E D W D D R
E O J S L G D G R L P L E H X I T I A V
M I K V H L Q E B Z A M R Q S Q M Z K
P S R D Z W M A J C X I C O U P K I E F
H U A E S B P U I E E R E N I O C N D T
A L S S P L S D R S C P I G S S D I U S
T C P A A R L U I K D T V T I I E S N J
I N I P V Y I C C E Y M E C T T S H A M
C O N T F L E E T C J S W D E I Z N J
A C G I T R T A V W E D U J W O G Q I Y
L C L T P O E P B E E S Q B L N N G M X
L N J U H M R T G D M U S Z T N A X O B
Y T M D R G A R E T J O F O C L T D U G
S E R E N E E P E C O N T O R T E D S S
P B P R T G M U P N U I F C C T D E E J
D H N F A I G K F R T M G R I B E G V B
C I H U F A C Q T Q E O C B I T X R I L
H Q S N V G K U E C M H I A E G M U T R
L S I T X K R C L W R H E L P W I S I D
A T U J R I N A M O O I O N B A D D G S
L V G R N A C M V R U S N W S E C B U L
X J N G H F U H P E B S Z G G I N I F G
W J A N C C T G A O L M L R E L V I T Z
W R E T C H E D H O H Y S Y W D K E G Y
E X U B E R A N T T S E X E M P T E D N
```

ANGUISH	DAZED	EXUBERANT	OMINOUS	SERENE
APPREHENSIVE	DEJECTED	FRIGID	PALPABLE	SUBTLE
APTITUDE	DESIGNATED	FUGITIVES	PERCEIVE	SUCCESSOR
ASSUAGE	DIMINISH	GRAVELY	PERMEATED	SURGED
BENIGN	DISPOSITION	IMPEDED	PLACIDLY	THRONG
CAPACITY	DISTRAUGHT	INFRINGED	PRECISE	TORRENT
CHAOS	EMPHATICALLY	METICULOUSLY	PRIMLY	UNANIMOUS
CONCLUSION	ENHANCE	MURKY	PROHIBITED	VAGUE
CONTORTED	EXEMPTED	NURTURING	RASPING	WRETCHED
CRINGED	EXQUISITE	OBSOLETE	REPRIEVE	

The Giver Vocabulary Word Search 4 Answer Key

ANGUISH	DAZED	EXUBERANT	OMINOUS	SERENE
APPREHENSIVE	DEJECTED	FRIGID	PALPABLE	SUBTLE
APTITUDE	DESIGNATED	FUGITIVES	PERCEIVE	SUCCESSOR
ASSUAGE	DIMINISH	GRAVELY	PERMEATED	SURGED
BENIGN	DISPOSITION	IMPEDED	PLACIDLY	THRONG
CAPACITY	DISTRAUGHT	INFRINGED	PRECISE	TORRENT
CHAOS	EMPHATICALLY	METICULOUSLY	PRIMLY	UNANIMOUS
CONCLUSION	ENHANCE	MURKY	PROHIBITED	VAGUE
CONTORTED	EXEMPTED	NURTURING	RASPING	WRETCHED
CRINGED	EXQUISITE	OBSOLETE	REPRIEVE	

The Giver Vocabulary Crossword 1

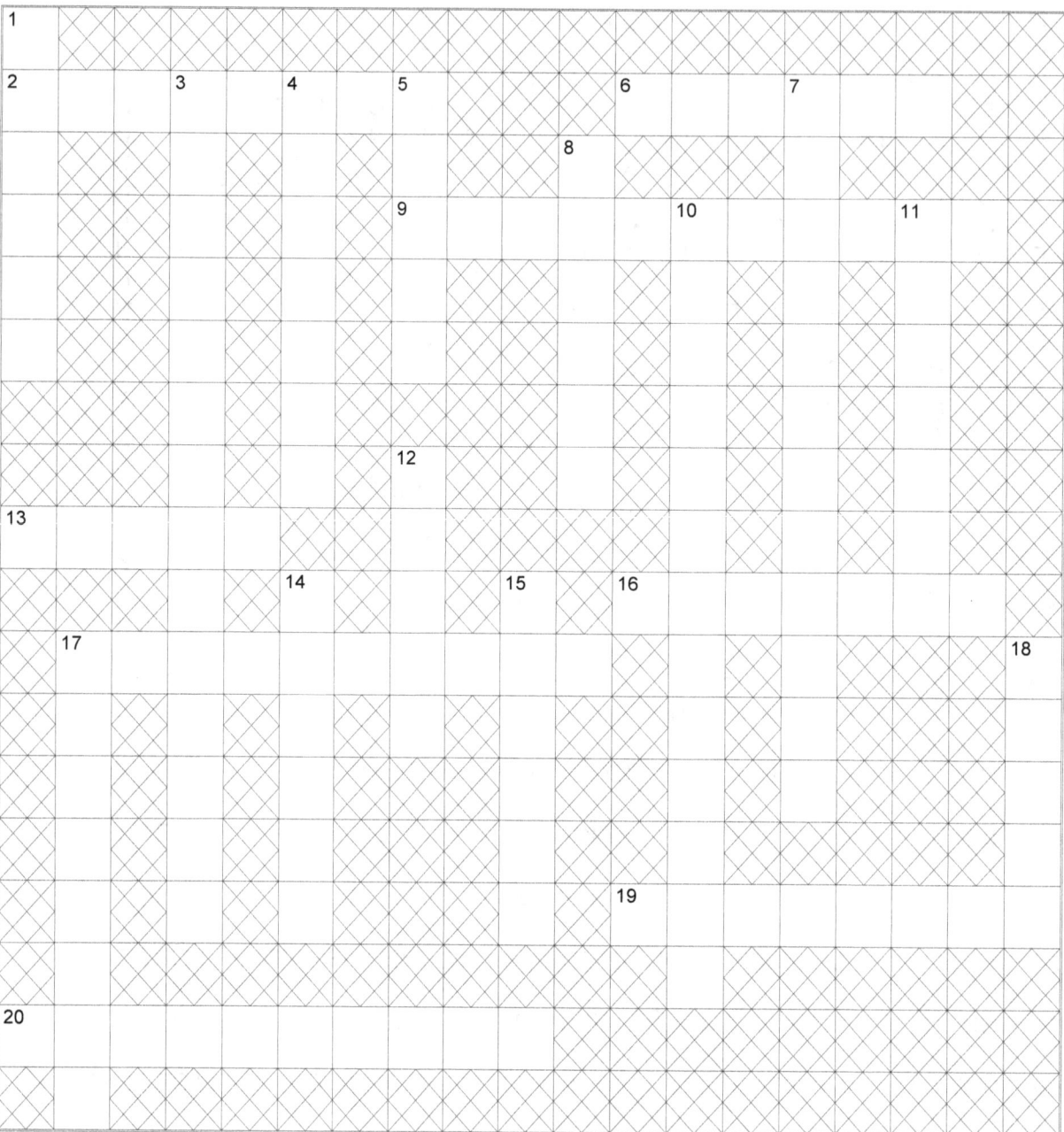

Across
2. Overjoyed
6. In a proper manner
9. Purchase
13. Stunned; bewildered
16. Distress; suffering
17. Very upset; agitated
19. Peacefully
20. In an ill-tempered way

Down
1. Harmless
3. Violations of laws or rules
4. Heavy downpour
5. Disorderly confusion
7. Extremely concerned with details
8. Indirect; faint
10. Unrehearsed
11. Threatening
12. Indefinite
14. Very cold
15. Crowd
17. Depressed
18. Dark; muddy; not clear

The Giver Vocabulary Crossword 1 Answer Key

	1 B										
2 E	C	3 S T	A	4 T	I	5 C		6 P	R	7 I M	L	Y
N		R		O		H	8 S			E	
I		A		R	9 A	C	Q	U	I	10 S	I	T	I	11 O	N
G		N		R		O		B		P		I		M
N		S		E		S		T		O		C		I
		G		N				L		N		U		N
		R		T		12 V		E		T		L		O
13 D	A	Z	E	D		A				A		O		U
				14 F		G	15 T	16 A	N	G	U	I	S	H
	17 D	I	S	T	R	A	U	G	H	T		E		S		18 M
	E			I		I		E		R		O		L		U
	J			O		G		E		O		U		Y		R
	E			N		I				N		S				K
	C			S		D				G	19 P	L	A	C	I	D	L	Y
	T										Y
20 P	E	T	U	L	A	N	T	L	Y
	D

Across
2. Overjoyed
6. In a proper manner
9. Purchase
13. Stunned; bewildered
16. Distress; suffering
17. Very upset; agitated
19. Peacefully
20. In an ill-tempered way

Down
1. Harmless
3. Violations of laws or rules
4. Heavy downpour
5. Disorderly confusion
7. Extremely concerned with details
8. Indirect; faint
10. Unrehearsed
11. Threatening
12. Indefinite
14. Very cold
15. Crowd
17. Depressed
18. Dark; muddy; not clear

The Giver Vocabulary Crossword 2

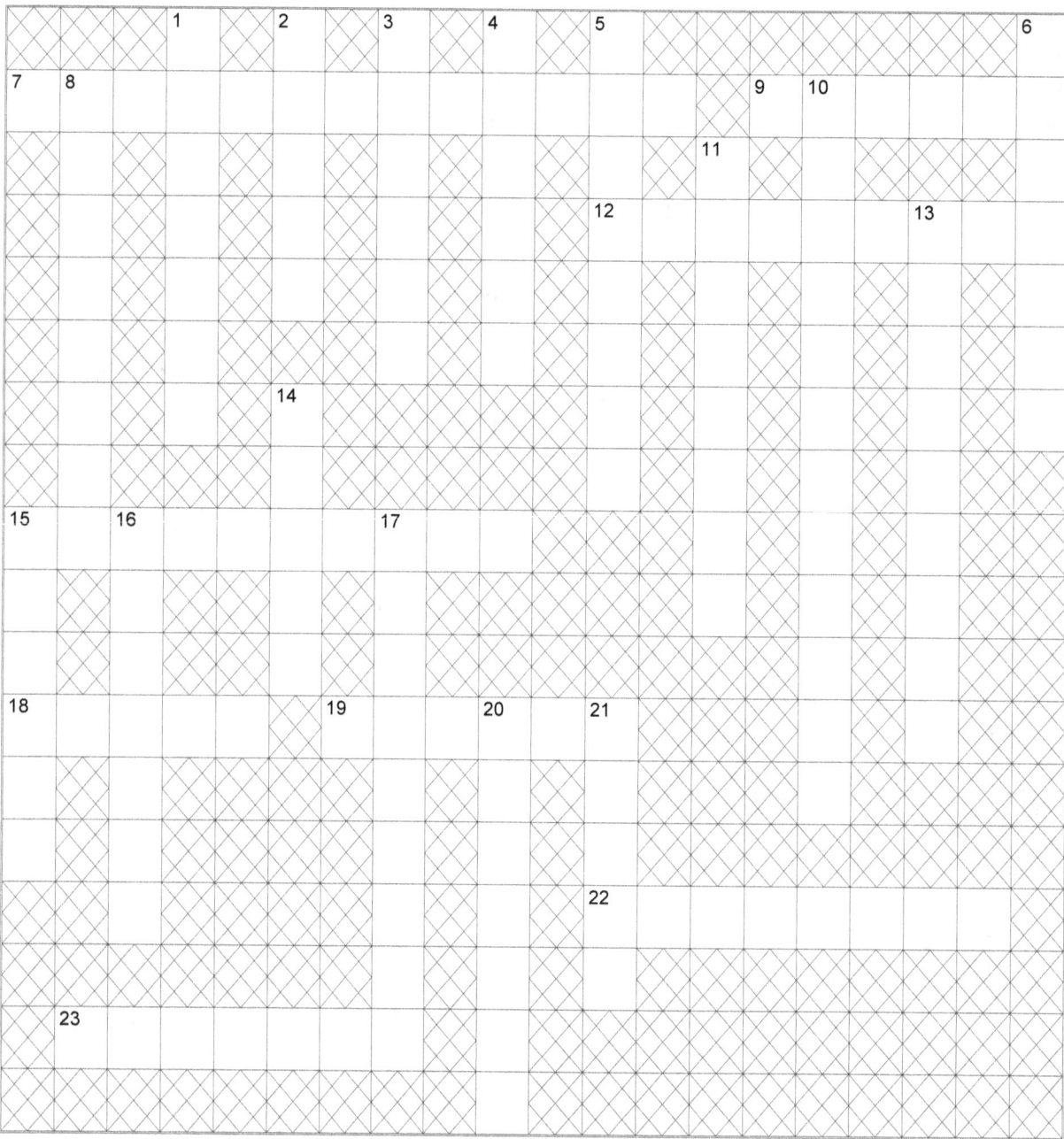

Across
7. Unrehearsed
9. Calm
12. Gradual increase in volume
15. In an ill-tempered way
18. Dark; muddy; not clear
19. Increased suddenly
22. Overjoyed
23. Got in the way of progress

Down
1. Distress; suffering
2. Indefinite
3. Harmless
4. Indirect; faint
5. Peacefully
6. Regret
8. Easily perceived; obvious
10. Agonizing
11. Depressed
13. Helping to grow or develop
14. Disorderly confusion
15. In a proper manner
16. Heavy downpour
17. Recorded and filed
20. Requiring serious thought
21. Stunned; bewildered

The Giver Vocabulary Crossword 2 Answer Key

		1 A	2 V	3 B		4 S		5 P			6 R
7 S	8 P	O	N	T	A	N	E	O	U	S	L	Y		9 S	10 E	R	E	N	E
	A	G	G		N		B		A	11 D		X		M
	L	U	U		I		T	12 C	R	E	S	C	13 E	N	D	O
	P	I	E		G		L	I		J		R	U		R
	A	S			N		E	D		E		U	R		S
	B	H	14 C					L		C		C	T		E
	L		H					Y		T		I	U	
15 P	E	16 T	U	L	A	17 N	T	L	Y		E		A	R
R		O		O		A					D		T	I
I		R		S		B							I	N
18 M	U	R	K	Y		19 S	U	R	20 G	E	21 D		N	G
L		E				L			R		A		G
Y		N				A			A		Z
		T				T			V		22 E	C	S	T	A	T	I	C
						E			E		D
	23 I	M	P	E	D	E	D		L
									Y

Across
7. Unrehearsed
9. Calm
12. Gradual increase in volume
15. In an ill-tempered way
18. Dark; muddy; not clear
19. Increased suddenly
22. Overjoyed
23. Got in the way of progress

Down
1. Distress; suffering
2. Indefinite
3. Harmless
4. Indirect; faint
5. Peacefully
6. Regret
8. Easily perceived; obvious
10. Agonizing
11. Depressed
13. Helping to grow or develop
14. Disorderly confusion
15. In a proper manner
16. Heavy downpour
17. Recorded and filed
20. Requiring serious thought
21. Stunned; bewildered

The Giver Vocabulary Crossword 3

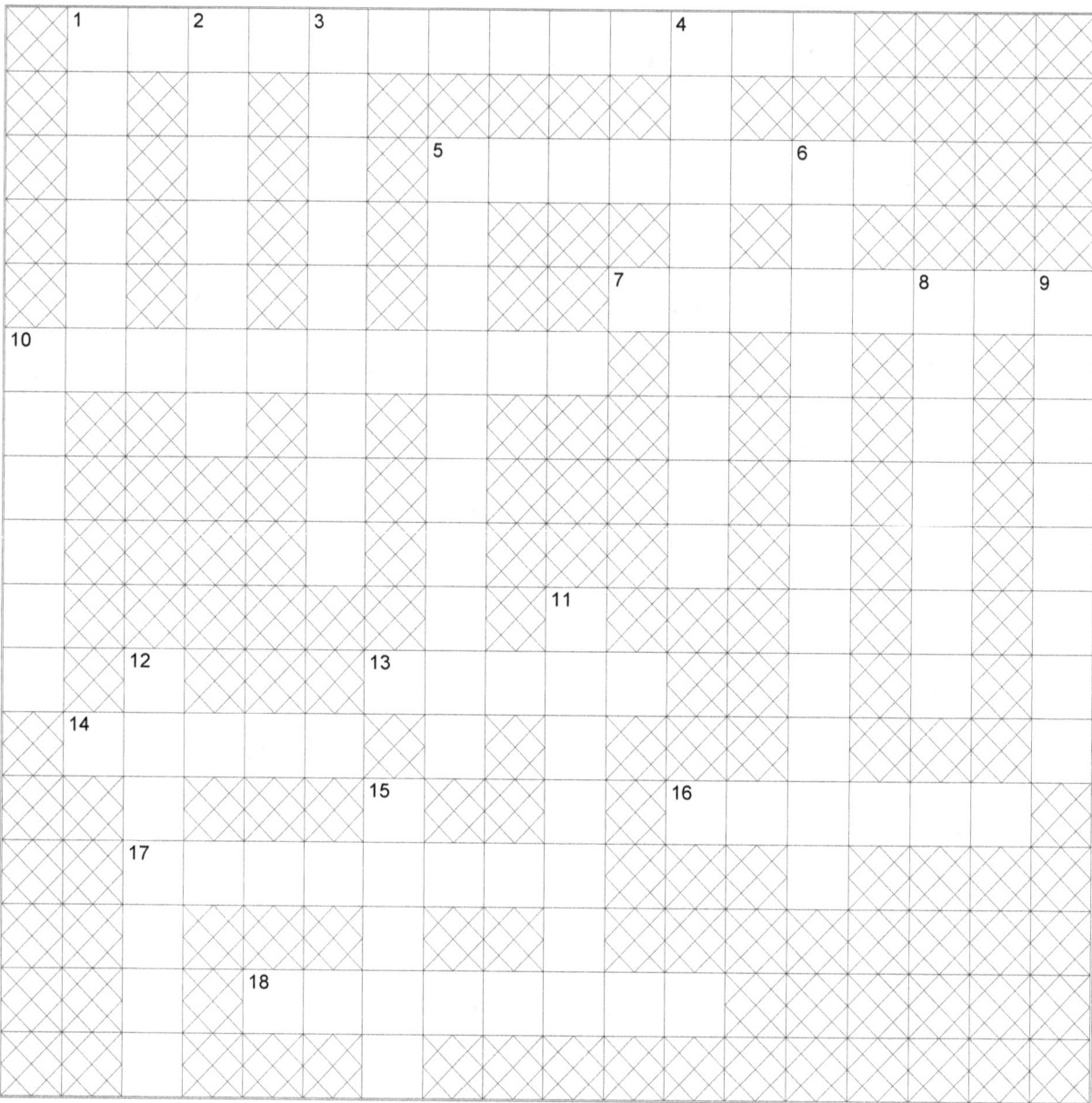

Across
1. Unrehearsed
5. Depressed
7. Become aware of through the senses
10. In an ill-tempered way
13. Disorderly confusion
14. Indefinite
16. Harmless
17. Easily perceived; obvious
18. Excluded from obligation

Down
1. Indirect; faint
2. Threatening
3. Recorded and filed
4. One who comes next
5. Very upset; agitated
6. Agonizing
8. Got in the way of progress
9. Overjoyed
10. In a proper manner
11. Heavy downpour
12. With a harsh, grating sound
15. Stunned; bewildered

The Giver Vocabulary Crossword 3 Answer Key

Across
1. Unrehearsed
5. Depressed
7. Become aware of through the senses
10. In an ill-tempered way
13. Disorderly confusion
14. Indefinite
16. Harmless
17. Easily perceived; obvious
18. Excluded from obligation

6. Agonizing
8. Got in the way of progress
9. Overjoyed
10. In a proper manner
11. Heavy downpour
12. With a harsh, grating sound
15. Stunned; bewildered

Down
1. Indirect; faint
2. Threatening
3. Recorded and filed
4. One who comes next
5. Very upset; agitated

The Giver Vocabulary Crossword 4

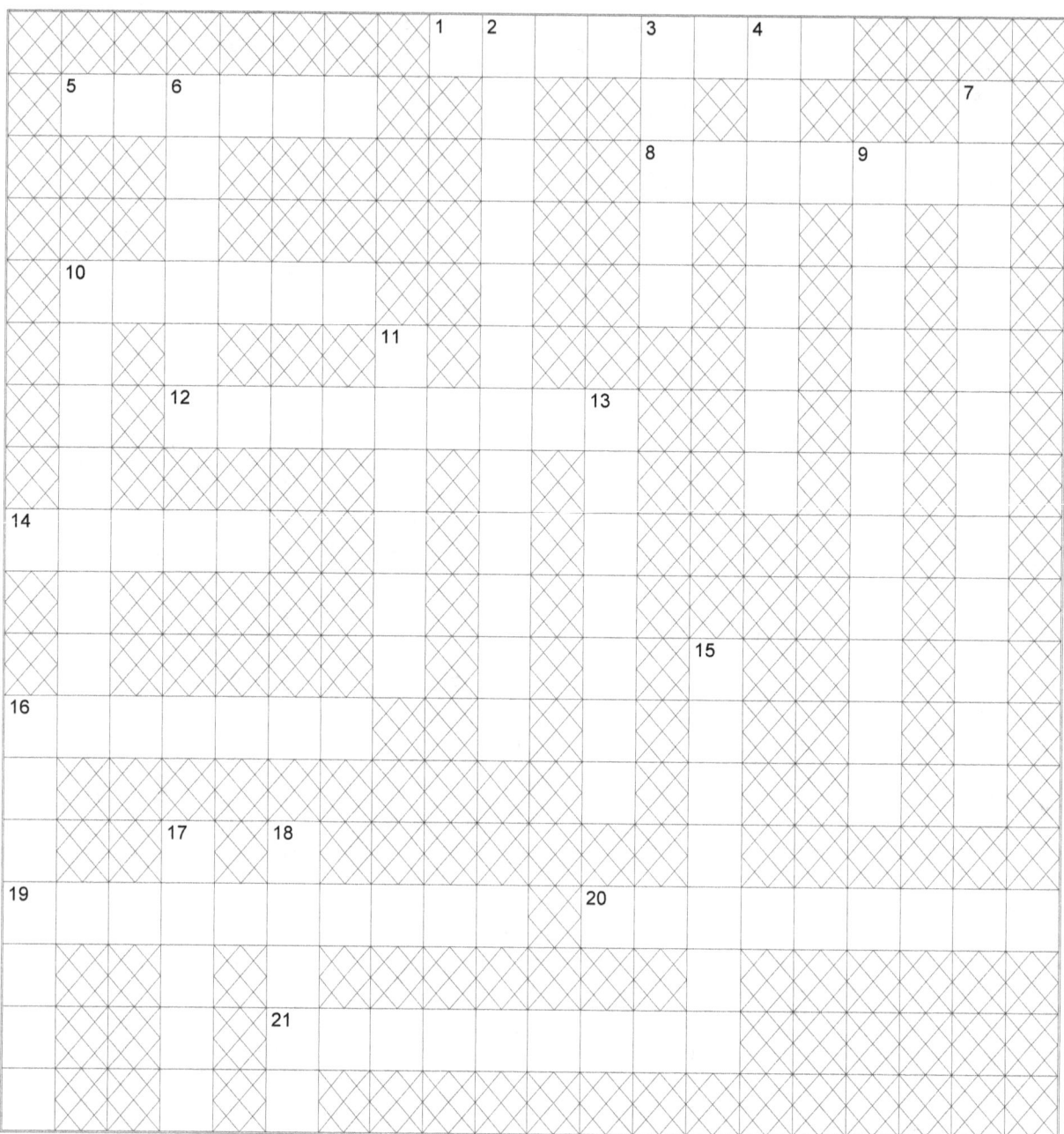

Across
1. Depressed
5. Indirect; faint
8. To relieve
10. In a proper manner
12. Helping to grow or develop
14. Indefinite
16. Regret
19. In an ill-tempered way
20. Gradual increase in volume
21. Done with a minimum of waste

Down
2. Agonizing
3. Disorderly confusion
4. Overjoyed
6. Harmless
7. Extremely concerned with details
9. Purchase
10. Easily perceived; obvious
11. Increased suddenly
13. Requiring serious thought
15. Heavy downpour
16. With a harsh, grating sound
17. Dark; muddy; not clear
18. Stunned; bewildered

The Giver Vocabulary Crossword 4 Answer Key

						1	2		3		4			
						D	E	J	E	C	T	E	D	
	5		6											7
	S	U	B	T	L	E			X		C			M
			E						C		8		9	
											A	S	S	U	A	G	E
			N						R		O		C		T
	10													
	P	R	I	M	L	Y			U		S		A		Q		I
			A				11		C				T		U		C
			G				S				13				
			12								G		I		I		U
			L	N	U	R	T	U	R	I	N	G		
			P				R		A		R		C		S		L
14														
V	A	G	U	E			G		T		A			I		O
			B				E		I		V		15		
													T		
			L				D		N		E		T		I		S
16														
R	E	M	O	R	S	E			G		L		O		O		L
A									Y		R				N		Y
S			17		18						R			
19			M		D				20					
P	E	T	U	L	A	N	T	L	Y	C	R	E	S	C	E	N	D	O
I			R		Z						N			
N			K		21									
					E	F	F	I	C	I	E	N	T	
G			Y		D									

Across
1. Depressed
5. Indirect; faint
8. To relieve
10. In a proper manner
12. Helping to grow or develop
14. Indefinite
16. Regret
19. In an ill-tempered way
20. Gradual increase in volume
21. Done with a minimum of waste

Down
2. Agonizing
3. Disorderly confusion
4. Overjoyed
6. Harmless
7. Extremely concerned with details
9. Purchase
10. Easily perceived; obvious
11. Increased suddenly
13. Requiring serious thought
15. Heavy downpour
16. With a harsh, grating sound
17. Dark; muddy; not clear
18. Stunned; bewildered

The Giver Vocabulary Juggle Letters 1

1. BSULTE = 1. _____
   Indirect; faint

2. NTETYVLITAE = 2. _____
   Uncertainly; with hesitation

3. UEANLTYLPT = 3. _____
   In an ill-tempered way

4. ODSONITSIIP = 4. _____
   Personality

5. LNIITAVG = 5. _____
   Alert; watchful

6. APISRNG = 6. _____
   With a harsh, grating sound

7. IUTETPAD = 7. _____
   Talent

8. TEFENCIIF = 8. _____
   Done with a minimum of waste

9. PMEDDEI = 9. _____
   Got in the way of progress

10. BOSETELO =10. _____
    No longer in use

11. TUEDABALT =11. _____
    Recorded and filed

12. OMIOSNU =12. _____
    Threatening

13. RUUINRNTG =13. _____
    Helping to grow or develop

14. IRLEHATXAE =14. _____
    Cause to feel energetic

15. ITYECLMPHAAL =15. _____
    Forcefully

The Giver Vocabulary Juggle Letters 1 Answer Key

1. BSULTE = 1. SUBTLE
   Indirect; faint

2. NTETYVLITAE = 2. TENTATIVELY
   Uncertainly; with hesitation

3. UEANLTYLPT = 3. PETULANTLY
   In an ill-tempered way

4. ODSONITSIIP = 4. DISPOSITION
   Personality

5. LNIITAVG = 5. VIGILANT
   Alert; watchful

6. APISRNG = 6. RASPING
   With a harsh, grating sound

7. IUTETPAD = 7. APTITUDE
   Talent

8. TEFENCIIF = 8. EFFICIENT
   Done with a minimum of waste

9. PMEDDEI = 9. IMPEDED
   Got in the way of progress

10. BOSETELO = 10. OBSOLETE
    No longer in use

11. TUEDABALT = 11. TABULATED
    Recorded and filed

12. OMIOSNU = 12. OMINOUS
    Threatening

13. RUUINRNTG = 13. NURTURING
    Helping to grow or develop

14. IRLEHATXAE = 14. EXHILARATE
    Cause to feel energetic

15. ITYECLMPHAAL = 15. EMPHATICALLY
    Forcefully

The Giver Vocabulary Juggle Letters 2

1. NTFEIFCIE = 1. _____
   Done with a minimum of waste

2. MNOISUO = 2. _____
   Threatening

3. EETSXQIIU = 3. _____
   Lovely

4. UNTIRGURN = 4. _____
   Helping to grow or develop

5. IRAXTEEHLA = 5. _____
   Cause to feel energetic

6. TAESCICT = 6. _____
   Overjoyed

7. RPILMY = 7. _____
   In a proper manner

8. ITUAPEDT = 8. _____
   Talent

9. NNCEEHA = 9. _____
   Improve

10. ROTCDTEON =10. _____
    Twisted; disfigured

11. NNIDAIOTMO =11. _____
    A reminder of a forgotten task or duty

12. SAHNGIU =12. _____
    Distress; suffering

13. LACYDILP =13. _____
    Peacefully

14. GRFIDI =14. _____
    Very cold

15. PPEVASNEIEHR =15. _____
    Fearful; anxious

The Giver Vocabulary Juggle Letters 2 Answer Key

1. NTFEIFCIE = 1. EFFICIENT
Done with a minimum of waste

2. MNOISUO = 2. OMINOUS
Threatening

3. EETSXQIIU = 3. EXQUISITE
Lovely

4. UNTIRGURN = 4. NURTURING
Helping to grow or develop

5. IRAXTEEHLA = 5. EXHILARATE
Cause to feel energetic

6. TAESCICT = 6. ECSTATIC
Overjoyed

7. RPILMY = 7. PRIMLY
In a proper manner

8. ITUAPEDT = 8. APTITUDE
Talent

9. NNCEEHA = 9. ENHANCE
Improve

10. ROTCDTEON = 10. CONTORTED
Twisted; disfigured

11. NNIDAIOTMO = 11. ADMONITION
A reminder of a forgotten task or duty

12. SAHNGIU = 12. ANGUISH
Distress; suffering

13. LACYDILP = 13. PLACIDLY
Peacefully

14. GRFIDI = 14. FRIGID
Very cold

15. PPEVASNEIEHR = 15. APPREHENSIVE
Fearful; anxious

The Giver Vocabulary Juggle Letters 3

1. GERNATUXCICI = 1. _____
Agonizing

2. SAUONITCIQI = 2. _____
Purchase

3. EVYETINLTAT = 3. _____
Uncertainly; with hesitation

4. EIICENTFF = 4. _____
Done with a minimum of waste

5. IPIOMTCSIT = 5. _____
Hopeful; expecting the best outcome

6. SGAEUAS = 6. _____
To relieve

7. GPSIRAN = 7. _____
With a harsh, grating sound

8. VEEIRREP = 8. _____
Pardon

9. CPSUUCINOSO = 9. _____
Noticeable

10. IYMRPL =10. _____
In a proper manner

11. UATLYNLPTE =11. _____
In an ill-tempered way

12. ISONLOCNUC =12. _____
The end

13. IPEERCS =13. _____
Exact

14. UCELSLTUYIMO =14. _____
Extremely concerned with details

15. PCATIYCA =15. _____
Ability to hold

The Giver Vocabulary Juggle Letters 3 Answer Key

1. GERNATUXCICI = 1. EXCRUCIATING
   Agonizing

2. SAUONITCIQI = 2. ACQUISITION
   Purchase

3. EVYETINLTAT = 3. TENTATIVELY
   Uncertainly; with hesitation

4. EIICENTFF = 4. EFFICIENT
   Done with a minimum of waste

5. IPIOMTCSIT = 5. OPTIMISTIC
   Hopeful; expecting the best outcome

6. SGAEUAS = 6. ASSUAGE
   To relieve

7. GPSIRAN = 7. RASPING
   With a harsh, grating sound

8. VEEIRREP = 8. REPRIEVE
   Pardon

9. CPSUUCINOSO = 9. CONSPICUOUS
   Noticeable

10. IYMRPL =10. PRIMLY
    In a proper manner

11. UATLYNLPTE =11. PETULANTLY
    In an ill-tempered way

12. ISONLOCNUC =12. CONCLUSION
    The end

13. IPEERCS =13. PRECISE
    Exact

14. UCELSLTUYIMO =14. METICULOUSLY
    Extremely concerned with details

15. PCATIYCA =15. CAPACITY
    Ability to hold

The Giver Vocabulary Juggle Letters 4

1. IOSDPISNOIT   = 1. _____
                        Personality

2. RCIENGD   = 2. _____
                        Shrank back in fear

3. EUALTDBTA   = 3. _____
                        Recorded and filed

4. VRIPEREE   = 4. _____
                        Pardon

5. SOHCA   = 5. _____
                        Disorderly confusion

6. ACTICAYP   = 6. _____
                        Ability to hold

7. SHITSCENTEMA   = 7. _____
                        Punishment

8. LUTSBE   = 8. _____
                        Indirect; faint

9. ASCCTEIT   = 9. _____
                        Overjoyed

10. VPREICEE   =10. _____
                        Become aware of through the senses

11. GIFDRI   =11. _____
                        Very cold

12. MNONSUUAI   =12. _____
                        In complete agreement

13. GICRICEXTAUN   =13. _____
                        Agonizing

14. ELYNSUOSOATNP =14. _____
                        Unrehearsed

15. TMYALHIECPAL   =15. _____
                        Forcefully

The Giver Vocabulary Juggle Letters 4 Answer Key

1. IOSDPISNOIT = 1. DISPOSITION
   Personality

2. RCIENGD = 2. CRINGED
   Shrank back in fear

3. EUALTDBTA = 3. TABULATED
   Recorded and filed

4. VRIPEREE = 4. REPRIEVE
   Pardon

5. SOHCA = 5. CHAOS
   Disorderly confusion

6. ACTICAYP = 6. CAPACITY
   Ability to hold

7. SHITSCENTEMA = 7. CHASTISEMENT
   Punishment

8. LUTSBE = 8. SUBTLE
   Indirect; faint

9. ASCCTEIT = 9. ECSTATIC
   Overjoyed

10. VPREICEE =10. PERCEIVE
    Become aware of through the senses

11. GIFDRI =11. FRIGID
    Very cold

12. MNONSUUAI =12. UNANIMOUS
    In complete agreement

13. GICRICEXTAUN =13. EXCRUCIATING
    Agonizing

14. ELYNSUOSOATNP =14. SPONTANEOUSLY
    Unrehearsed

15. TMYALHIECPAL =15. EMPHATICALLY
    Forcefully

ACQUISITION	Purchase
ADMONITION	A reminder of a forgotten task or duty
ANGUISH	Distress; suffering
APPARENT	Visible; easily seen
APPREHENSIVE	Fearful; anxious
APTITUDE	Talent

ASSUAGE	To relieve
BENIGN	Harmless
CAPACITY	Ability to hold
CHAOS	Disorderly confusion
CHASTISEMENT	Punishment
CONCLUSION	The end

CONSPICUOUS	Noticeable
CONTORTED	Twisted; disfigured
CRESCENDO	Gradual increase in volume
CRINGED	Shrank back in fear
DAZED	Stunned; bewildered
DEJECTED	Depressed

DESIGNATED	Indicated; pointed out
DIMINISH	Decrease
DISPOSITION	Personality
DISTRAUGHT	Very upset; agitated
ECSTATIC	Overjoyed
EFFICIENT	Done with a minimum of waste

EMPHATICALLY	Forcefully
ENHANCE	Improve
EXCRUCIATING	Agonizing
EXEMPTED	Excluded from obligation
EXHILARATE	Cause to feel energetic
EXQUISITE	Lovely

EXUBERANT	High-spirited
FRIGID	Very cold
FUGITIVES	People running away
GRAVELY	Requiring serious thought
IMPEDED	Got in the way of progress
INFRINGED	Intruded

INVIGORATING	Refreshing; stimulating
METICULOUSLY	Extremely concerned with details
MURKY	Dark; muddy; not clear
NURTURING	Helping to grow or develop
OBSOLETE	No longer in use
OMINOUS	Threatening

OPTIMISTIC	Hopeful; expecting the best outcome
PALPABLE	Easily perceived; obvious
PERCEIVE	Become aware of through the senses
PERMEATED	Spread or flowing throughout
PETULANTLY	In an ill-tempered way
PLACIDLY	Peacefully

PRECISE	Exact
PRIMLY	In a proper manner
PROHIBITED	Forbidden
RASPING	With a harsh, grating sound
REMORSE	Regret
REPRIEVE	Pardon

SERENE	Calm
SPONTANEOUSLY	Unrehearsed
SUBTLE	Indirect; faint
SUCCESSOR	One who comes next
SURGED	Increased suddenly
TABULATED	Recorded and filed

TENTATIVELY	Uncertainly; with hesitation
THRONG	Crowd
TORRENT	Heavy downpour
TRANSGRESSIONS	Violations of laws or rules
UNANIMOUS	In complete agreement
VAGUE	Indefinite

VIGILANT	Alert; watchful
WRETCHED	Miserable

The Giver Vocabulary

SERENE	NURTURING	ANGUISH	ADMONITION	SUCCESSOR
APPARENT	EXEMPTED	EXUBERANT	FRIGID	CHASTISEMENT
EXCRUCIATING	SPONTANEOUSLY	FREE SPACE	GRAVELY	REPRIEVE
ACQUISITION	METICULOUSLY	CONSPICUOUS	EMPHATICALLY	CRINGED
DESIGNATED	TRANSGRESSIONS	CONCLUSION	THRONG	OBSOLETE

The Giver Vocabulary

SUBTLE	ENHANCE	CRESCENDO	SURGED	WRETCHED
INFRINGED	IMPEDED	APTITUDE	OMINOUS	TABULATED
UNANIMOUS	DIMINISH	FREE SPACE	CAPACITY	TORRENT
DISPOSITION	PERMEATED	PRIMLY	RASPING	CONTORTED
BENIGN	FUGITIVES	TENTATIVELY	EXHILARATE	PETULANTLY

The Giver Vocabulary

APPREHENSIVE	TORRENT	SPONTANEOUSLY	APPARENT	DEJECTED
PROHIBITED	REPRIEVE	CRESCENDO	EFFICIENT	PALPABLE
CHAOS	SERENE	FREE SPACE	OBSOLETE	WRETCHED
ACQUISITION	THRONG	PLACIDLY	TABULATED	OMINOUS
FUGITIVES	UNANIMOUS	DIMINISH	APTITUDE	INFRINGED

The Giver Vocabulary

CONTORTED	CRINGED	ECSTATIC	EXHILARATE	FRIGID
PRIMLY	PETULANTLY	TRANSGRESSIONS	CHASTISEMENT	ASSUAGE
OPTIMISTIC	PERCEIVE	FREE SPACE	INVIGORATING	RASPING
BENIGN	METICULOUSLY	TENTATIVELY	REMORSE	GRAVELY
EXUBERANT	ENHANCE	CONSPICUOUS	CONCLUSION	VAGUE

The Giver Vocabulary

SURGED	ENHANCE	DESIGNATED	ACQUISITION	CAPACITY
UNANIMOUS	PRECISE	ECSTATIC	TORRENT	OBSOLETE
FUGITIVES	EXEMPTED	FREE SPACE	RASPING	OPTIMISTIC
CHASTISEMENT	IMPEDED	PERCEIVE	FRIGID	PERMEATED
MURKY	VIGILANT	THRONG	CRESCENDO	ADMONITION

The Giver Vocabulary

DIMINISH	OMINOUS	EFFICIENT	SUBTLE	CHAOS
CONTORTED	APTITUDE	DEJECTED	ASSUAGE	TABULATED
REPRIEVE	TRANSGRESSIONS	FREE SPACE	EXHILARATE	EXQUISITE
DAZED	INVIGORATING	PRIMLY	TENTATIVELY	DISTRAUGHT
APPARENT	DISPOSITION	REMORSE	PALPABLE	WRETCHED

The Giver Vocabulary

INFRINGED	CHASTISEMENT	CONTORTED	RASPING	APPARENT
PRIMLY	ANGUISH	CAPACITY	PERCEIVE	MURKY
NURTURING	ADMONITION	FREE SPACE	OMINOUS	TORRENT
OBSOLETE	EMPHATICALLY	EFFICIENT	DESIGNATED	WRETCHED
INVIGORATING	PROHIBITED	METICULOUSLY	CONCLUSION	PETULANTLY

The Giver Vocabulary

APTITUDE	REPRIEVE	FRIGID	REMORSE	ASSUAGE
CRINGED	DISPOSITION	UNANIMOUS	SUBTLE	CRESCENDO
ACQUISITION	SURGED	FREE SPACE	VIGILANT	ENHANCE
BENIGN	EXQUISITE	CHAOS	FUGITIVES	OPTIMISTIC
CONSPICUOUS	IMPEDED	DAZED	EXUBERANT	THRONG

The Giver Vocabulary

CRINGED	TORRENT	ASSUAGE	INVIGORATING	CHAOS
OMINOUS	ADMONITION	OBSOLETE	FRIGID	PERMEATED
PERCEIVE	METICULOUSLY	FREE SPACE	APPARENT	EXQUISITE
TABULATED	EFFICIENT	ECSTATIC	EMPHATICALLY	PETULANTLY
UNANIMOUS	VAGUE	APTITUDE	GRAVELY	APPREHENSIVE

The Giver Vocabulary

DAZED	CONSPICUOUS	MURKY	EXCRUCIATING	EXHILARATE
OPTIMISTIC	TRANSGRESSIONS	DISTRAUGHT	CHASTISEMENT	FUGITIVES
SERENE	REPRIEVE	FREE SPACE	PROHIBITED	DEJECTED
SUBTLE	RASPING	EXEMPTED	BENIGN	REMORSE
IMPEDED	DIMINISH	PRECISE	CONCLUSION	SUCCESSOR

The Giver Vocabulary

FUGITIVES	PETULANTLY	EMPHATICALLY	ASSUAGE	PRIMLY
EXUBERANT	CHAOS	TRANSGRESSIONS	EXEMPTED	OMINOUS
SERENE	REMORSE	FREE SPACE	ANGUISH	CONTORTED
VIGILANT	CONCLUSION	DISTRAUGHT	INFRINGED	MURKY
ADMONITION	SURGED	VAGUE	APPREHENSIVE	PALPABLE

The Giver Vocabulary

GRAVELY	OPTIMISTIC	THRONG	OBSOLETE	PRECISE
PERMEATED	EXQUISITE	PROHIBITED	BENIGN	CAPACITY
DEJECTED	PERCEIVE	FREE SPACE	EFFICIENT	TENTATIVELY
SUBTLE	TABULATED	APPARENT	ENHANCE	DIMINISH
DISPOSITION	ACQUISITION	CRINGED	WRETCHED	CONSPICUOUS

The Giver Vocabulary

SUCCESSOR	TRANSGRESSIONS	APPARENT	REMORSE	TABULATED
INFRINGED	CRESCENDO	DISPOSITION	MURKY	DIMINISH
EXCRUCIATING	DISTRAUGHT	FREE SPACE	ECSTATIC	EFFICIENT
CONSPICUOUS	METICULOUSLY	PROHIBITED	EXHILARATE	PETULANTLY
TORRENT	OBSOLETE	IMPEDED	CONTORTED	TENTATIVELY

The Giver Vocabulary

CONCLUSION	CAPACITY	ADMONITION	PERMEATED	PRIMLY
VAGUE	DEJECTED	EXQUISITE	NURTURING	ACQUISITION
EXEMPTED	BENIGN	FREE SPACE	SUBTLE	SURGED
PLACIDLY	CHASTISEMENT	ASSUAGE	ENHANCE	DESIGNATED
GRAVELY	EMPHATICALLY	REPRIEVE	ANGUISH	FRIGID

The Giver Vocabulary

CHAOS	SUBTLE	TRANSGRESSIONS	DEJECTED	DIMINISH
CHASTISEMENT	TORRENT	ADMONITION	APPREHENSIVE	CAPACITY
IMPEDED	EFFICIENT	FREE SPACE	SERENE	EXCRUCIATING
SPONTANEOUSLY	PERMEATED	ASSUAGE	DAZED	GRAVELY
DISTRAUGHT	TABULATED	PERCEIVE	PROHIBITED	DISPOSITION

The Giver Vocabulary

CONTORTED	VIGILANT	EXHILARATE	EMPHATICALLY	NURTURING
INFRINGED	PLACIDLY	FUGITIVES	APTITUDE	PALPABLE
METICULOUSLY	EXQUISITE	FREE SPACE	PRECISE	UNANIMOUS
CRESCENDO	VAGUE	WRETCHED	RASPING	CONCLUSION
SUCCESSOR	TENTATIVELY	PRIMLY	OPTIMISTIC	EXUBERANT

The Giver Vocabulary

ANGUISH	DEJECTED	CHASTISEMENT	SPONTANEOUSLY	DAZED
VAGUE	REPRIEVE	TRANSGRESSIONS	CONCLUSION	PALPABLE
ENHANCE	CHAOS	FREE SPACE	INFRINGED	SURGED
DISTRAUGHT	CRINGED	GRAVELY	REMORSE	TENTATIVELY
WRETCHED	APTITUDE	THRONG	SUCCESSOR	IMPEDED

The Giver Vocabulary

BENIGN	SUBTLE	EXEMPTED	EXUBERANT	ECSTATIC
PLACIDLY	PRECISE	UNANIMOUS	DESIGNATED	EXHILARATE
DISPOSITION	PERCEIVE	FREE SPACE	PROHIBITED	FRIGID
ASSUAGE	MURKY	EFFICIENT	PRIMLY	OBSOLETE
ACQUISITION	FUGITIVES	PERMEATED	TORRENT	OMINOUS

The Giver Vocabulary

PALPABLE	ACQUISITION	REMORSE	PRECISE	ADMONITION
UNANIMOUS	FUGITIVES	WRETCHED	ANGUISH	BENIGN
DIMINISH	EXHILARATE	FREE SPACE	INFRINGED	PERCEIVE
TRANSGRESSIONS	CONTORTED	CHASTISEMENT	TABULATED	CAPACITY
METICULOUSLY	DISTRAUGHT	DESIGNATED	SUCCESSOR	PRIMLY

The Giver Vocabulary

EXEMPTED	REPRIEVE	APPREHENSIVE	OBSOLETE	THRONG
RASPING	DISPOSITION	ECSTATIC	PETULANTLY	CONCLUSION
PERMEATED	NURTURING	FREE SPACE	CRINGED	SUBTLE
CONSPICUOUS	ASSUAGE	INVIGORATING	PROHIBITED	MURKY
EMPHATICALLY	CRESCENDO	TENTATIVELY	VIGILANT	CHAOS

The Giver Vocabulary

CONCLUSION	PRECISE	OMINOUS	DIMINISH	INFRINGED
TENTATIVELY	PETULANTLY	OBSOLETE	REPRIEVE	CHASTISEMENT
DEJECTED	OPTIMISTIC	FREE SPACE	EXCRUCIATING	FUGITIVES
EXEMPTED	PRIMLY	APTITUDE	APPREHENSIVE	FRIGID
VAGUE	VIGILANT	RASPING	APPARENT	PERMEATED

The Giver Vocabulary

ACQUISITION	EXQUISITE	WRETCHED	IMPEDED	EXHILARATE
SUCCESSOR	THRONG	TRANSGRESSIONS	BENIGN	ASSUAGE
ADMONITION	EFFICIENT	FREE SPACE	ANGUISH	EMPHATICALLY
PERCEIVE	METICULOUSLY	DAZED	SPONTANEOUSLY	PLACIDLY
ECSTATIC	CAPACITY	EXUBERANT	SERENE	ENHANCE

The Giver Vocabulary

CRINGED	REMORSE	PERMEATED	WRETCHED	THRONG
EXHILARATE	IMPEDED	APTITUDE	ACQUISITION	PETULANTLY
CHAOS	DAZED	FREE SPACE	FRIGID	ANGUISH
OPTIMISTIC	RASPING	VIGILANT	PROHIBITED	CHASTISEMENT
ENHANCE	REPRIEVE	ADMONITION	ECSTATIC	EXEMPTED

The Giver Vocabulary

PLACIDLY	TABULATED	DESIGNATED	DEJECTED	VAGUE
PRECISE	EXQUISITE	TORRENT	EXCRUCIATING	EXUBERANT
DISPOSITION	EMPHATICALLY	FREE SPACE	PERCEIVE	DIMINISH
CAPACITY	SUCCESSOR	SUBTLE	TRANSGRESSIONS	DISTRAUGHT
METICULOUSLY	OMINOUS	MURKY	PRIMLY	ASSUAGE

The Giver Vocabulary

PALPABLE	SUBTLE	INVIGORATING	TRANSGRESSIONS	IMPEDED
THRONG	BENIGN	CONSPICUOUS	SERENE	DISTRAUGHT
EXEMPTED	FRIGID	FREE SPACE	CRINGED	MURKY
TORRENT	SUCCESSOR	APTITUDE	DEJECTED	ADMONITION
FUGITIVES	DIMINISH	PROHIBITED	ANGUISH	CHASTISEMENT

The Giver Vocabulary

EXHILARATE	PRECISE	EXUBERANT	ASSUAGE	INFRINGED
OBSOLETE	OPTIMISTIC	PERMEATED	TENTATIVELY	CONCLUSION
APPREHENSIVE	APPARENT	FREE SPACE	OMINOUS	CHAOS
UNANIMOUS	CONTORTED	PERCEIVE	RASPING	SURGED
REMORSE	TABULATED	EMPHATICALLY	DESIGNATED	ACQUISITION

The Giver Vocabulary

METICULOUSLY	INFRINGED	MURKY	PETULANTLY	WRETCHED
PLACIDLY	DEJECTED	CONTORTED	CONSPICUOUS	EXQUISITE
PRIMLY	SUBTLE	FREE SPACE	VIGILANT	APPARENT
TENTATIVELY	INVIGORATING	EFFICIENT	VAGUE	ACQUISITION
CAPACITY	GRAVELY	THRONG	TORRENT	ADMONITION

The Giver Vocabulary

REPRIEVE	APPREHENSIVE	FUGITIVES	FRIGID	OBSOLETE
EXEMPTED	EMPHATICALLY	SPONTANEOUSLY	CONCLUSION	CHASTISEMENT
CRINGED	NURTURING	FREE SPACE	REMORSE	SURGED
SUCCESSOR	EXUBERANT	IMPEDED	PRECISE	PROHIBITED
SERENE	UNANIMOUS	BENIGN	CRESCENDO	EXCRUCIATING

The Giver Vocabulary

RASPING	EXUBERANT	CRINGED	EXEMPTED	MURKY
DIMINISH	NURTURING	THRONG	ENHANCE	APPARENT
APPREHENSIVE	APTITUDE	FREE SPACE	PRECISE	INVIGORATING
ADMONITION	CONTORTED	FUGITIVES	TRANSGRESSIONS	EXCRUCIATING
CHAOS	VAGUE	DEJECTED	TENTATIVELY	IMPEDED

The Giver Vocabulary

ASSUAGE	PERCEIVE	PLACIDLY	TABULATED	SURGED
GRAVELY	INFRINGED	TORRENT	REMORSE	CONSPICUOUS
BENIGN	PETULANTLY	FREE SPACE	SERENE	EMPHATICALLY
PERMEATED	DISTRAUGHT	DAZED	DESIGNATED	ECSTATIC
UNANIMOUS	METICULOUSLY	PROHIBITED	EXHILARATE	EXQUISITE

The Giver Vocabulary

PERMEATED	INVIGORATING	APPARENT	EXUBERANT	CAPACITY
GRAVELY	ADMONITION	CHAOS	ASSUAGE	TRANSGRESSIONS
VIGILANT	OPTIMISTIC	FREE SPACE	EXHILARATE	APPREHENSIVE
CONSPICUOUS	THRONG	EXQUISITE	ANGUISH	PERCEIVE
EXEMPTED	DIMINISH	DAZED	SUBTLE	OMINOUS

The Giver Vocabulary

MURKY	SERENE	PRECISE	DEJECTED	PLACIDLY
ENHANCE	ECSTATIC	PETULANTLY	TENTATIVELY	TORRENT
METICULOUSLY	EMPHATICALLY	FREE SPACE	OBSOLETE	SUCCESSOR
BENIGN	PRIMLY	NURTURING	PROHIBITED	PALPABLE
REPRIEVE	EXCRUCIATING	IMPEDED	FUGITIVES	WRETCHED

www.ingramcontent.com/pod-product-compliance
Lightning Source LLC
Chambersburg PA
CBHW081453070526
44586CB00019B/2341